from CLUELESS *to* CLASS ACT

MANNERS

for the

MODERN MAN

JODI R. R. SMITH

STERLING
New York

For my father, who taught me that just because life is not fair does not excuse us from being fair. For my husband, my willing foil, who really does know that two rudes do not make a right.

///////////////////

STERLING
New York

An Imprint of Sterling Publishing
1166 Avenue of the Americas
New York, NY 10036

STERLING and the distinctive Sterling logo are registered trademarks of Sterling Publishing Co., Inc.

This edition published in 2015

Revised text © 2015 by Jodi R. R. Smith
Previously published in 2004 by Sterling Publishing Company.
Text © 2004 by Jodi R. R. Smith. Illustrations © 2004 by Bill Reid

ISBN 978-1-4549-1640-6

Distributed in Canada by Sterling Publishing
℅ Canadian Manda Group, 664 Annette Street
Toronto, Ontario, Canada M6S 2C8
Distributed in the United Kingdom by GMC Distribution Services
Castle Place, 166 High Street, Lewes, East Sussex, England BN7 1XU
Distributed in Australia by Capricorn Link (Australia) Pty. Ltd.
P.O. Box 704, Windsor, NSW 2756, Australia

For information about custom editions, special sales, and premium and corporate purchases, please contact Sterling Special Sales at 800-805-5489 or specialsales@sterlingpublishing.com.

Manufactured in the United States of America

2 4 6 8 10 9 7 5 3 1

www.sterlingpublishing.com

CONTENTS

INTRODUCTION 5

CHAPTER ONE 7
PUBLIC PLACES
and EVENTS

CHAPTER TWO 25
the GENTLEMANLY
GUEST

CHAPTER THREE 39
the HOSPITABLE
HOST

CHAPTER FOUR 61
GRACIOUS DINING

CHAPTER FIVE 88
DATING DOS
and DON'TS

CHAPTER SIX 98
PERSONAL
APPEARANCE

CHAPTER SEVEN 111
MEETING *and*
GREETING

CHAPTER EIGHT 120
EVERYDAY *and*
EVERY-SO-OFTEN
ENCOUNTERS

CHAPTER NINE 129
HERE *to* THERE

CHAPTER TEN 139
TIPS *on* TIPPING

CHAPTER ELEVEN 145
KEEP *in* TOUCH

CHAPTER TWELVE 162
LIFE *at* WORK

CONCLUSION 174
INDEX 175

ACKNOWLEDGMENTS

This edition could not have come to be without the support and help of many polite people whose positive behavior has served as a beacon of civility, my family who know good manners is a journey and not necessarily a destination, my friends who bring me fabulous faux pas examples from their personal and professional lives, and the thousands of people who have participated in my seminars, written to me via the Web and engaged with me via social media.

INTRODUCTION

Have you ever noticed that there are some people to whom you take an instant liking? You enjoy speaking with them and look forward to seeing them again. Being with them actually makes you feel better about yourself. Conversely, there are those who make you feel uncomfortable whenever you're around them. While you may not be able to put your finger on the exact reason, as soon as you start talking to such a person, you wish that you were somewhere else. Often, these reactions are caused by the other individual's mastery of social guidelines.

Understanding how to behave in different situations is key to being a class act. The refined gentleman is comfortable in a variety of environments and is able to make those around him comfortable as well. While it may seem as though he has some inherent capability for knowing exactly how to behave in different situations and how to interact with different individuals, this is not the case. In fact, the big secret is that people are not born with charm; it is actually a learned skill. And it is not a difficult one. While etiquette may seem like a daunting subject, it's really quite simple, centering upon respect, consideration for others, and common sense. This means that with a bit of reading and a little practice, you too can know just what to say and do in all sorts of circumstances. You too can be a class act.

Becoming a class act is not only a relatively simple goal to achieve, but also an important one. Our abilities in a whole range of areas are generalized based upon the social behaviors we exhibit. Whether you are interviewing for a new job, building your business, or seeking new social relationships, *manners matter*.

This book contains a number of etiquette guidelines to help you navigate some of the most common interactions. Please note that I use the word "guidelines" deliberately. Contrary to popular belief, etiquette is not about rules. I never speak of etiquette in terms of rules because for every etiquette rule, I can think of an exception (or two or three). Guidelines allow for variation. Guidelines understand that behaviors are situationally specific. For instance, while you would of course use a fork and knife when dining out at a fancy restaurant, you wouldn't think twice about using your fingers when eating pizza with your family at home. It is important to understand not only what the etiquette guidelines are, but also when and how to apply them.

It is my hope that you will use this book in two ways. First, that you are enthralled enough to sit down with a refreshing drink and read it cover to cover. Second, that you will keep it on hand to refer to as etiquette issues arise. If you encounter etiquette emergencies outside of the topics covered in this book, please contact me via the Mannersmith website: www.mannersmith.com.

I hope you find this book both educational and entertaining.

///

CHAPTER ONE

PUBLIC PLACES *and* EVENTS

\\\

YOU MAY BE SURPRISED TO HEAR THAT it's alright to hang out in your sweatpants, watch television, and eat dinner from a take-out container—as long as you're home alone. Everyone, of course, needs a little downtime now and then to unwind. But if you plan to interact with others, this m.o. is not the best way to make friends or impress others. When hitting the town, you'll need to modify both your behavior and your clothes.

RESTAURANTS

DRESS TO DINE: Your clothing should match the formality of the restaurant. At some fine-dining establishments, you'll be required to wear a jacket and tie. Check the website or call ahead so that you're dressed appropriately.

AVOID THE WAIT: Whenever possible, make a reservation. Investing a few moments in this simple step could save you an hour or so once you actually arrive at the restaurant, which may not be able to accommodate you in a timely fashion without advance notice (in fact, some popular venues may not be able to seat you at all if you don't make a reservation). Some social media reservation sites will allow you to earn points toward priority seating or other dining perks.

HOLD YOUR HORSES: Even when you do have a reservation, there are instances in which you may still need to wait for your table (there are all sorts of unpredictable variables involved, and not all establishments have the timing down to an exact science). If you find yourself in this situation, visit the bar, take a walk around the block, or peruse the menu. If after fifteen minutes your table still isn't ready, ask the maître d'—in a respectful tone—how much longer he expects the wait to be. Do not make a scene, as this rarely helps.

DON'T FLASH THE CASH: In the movies and many sitcoms, the characters will wave some money beneath the nose of the maître d' to speed up the seating process. In real life, this rarely works. What's more, you'll simply be identifying yourself as a heathen since tipping is always done discreetly.

from CLUELESS *to* CLASS ACT

MAY I TAKE YOUR COAT? If you are with a date, a female relative, or an unescorted woman in a social situation and the restaurant has a coat check, ask this female companion if she'd like to check her coat. To help a woman take off this garment, stand behind her, gently but firmly grasp the shoulder seam of the coat with both hands, lift it up slightly above her shoulders, and then bring it down so that the sleeves slide off her arms. Fold the garment lengthwise, and hand it to the attendant. Note that when a woman is sporting a fur coat, she'll wear it to the table, take her seat, and shrug the fur off her shoulders onto the back of the chair. You should help her into her chair (see below), but she will shrug the coat off herself.

BAR BEHAVIOR: If your table is not ready and you decide to wait at the bar, you aren't obligated to order a drink, though you may receive a number of looks from the bartenders who count on tips for their income. If one person from your party orders a drink, everyone should. It is perfectly fine to order a soft drink, even if others are having alcoholic beverages. In finer establishments, if your table is called while you are still finishing your drink, a barkeep will carry it to your table for you. In more casual places, you will be expected to carry your own drink. While bartenders usually prefer that you settle your tab before sitting down to dinner, you may ask the waitstaff to include your bar balance in the final bill for the evening.

CHAIR CARE: When you are dining socially, it is a kind and gentlemanly gesture to help a woman (or your date) with her chair. Simply pull the chair out from the table, allow the woman to step in front of the chair, then gently push the chair forward until it touches the back of her knees; this is the signal that she should reach behind her for the chair while beginning to sit. As she starts to sit, continue to push the chair into the table. Once she is fully seated, one or two small adjustment pushes may be necessary to ensure that she is close enough to be able to eat easily, but not so close that her body is squished. To help a woman out of her chair, stand behind the chair and slowly pull it back until she has enough room to stand. Once she is up and away from the chair, push it back toward the table so that it does not block the path of other patrons.

COURSE FOR COURSE: Everyone at the table should order the same number of courses. It is awkward for some people to be eating while others aren't. Even if you aren't particularly hungry, you should match your companions course for course. It is the host's responsibility to ensure that everyone knows what, and how much, to order. If you are the host, you can accomplish this by commenting on what you are thinking of having, mentioning any starters as well as an entrée. If you are a guest and unsure what to order, simply ask the host: "This menu is wonderful, what do you plan to order?" Or, as the orders are being placed, listen to your companions' selections and match their courses. If you've ordered first only to find that others are having appetizers while you requested only an entrée, you can easily change your order: "Oh, that sounds good. I would also like a shrimp cocktail for an appetizer."

DRINK FOR DRINK: If others at your table are ordering drinks, you should order some type of refreshment as well, though it does not need to be an alcoholic beverage. Even if others are sipping wine or mixed drinks, it is perfectly

from CLUELESS *to* CLASS ACT

acceptable to order soda, sparkling water, or some other nonalcoholic beverage. (For more information regarding etiquette and alcoholic beverages, see page 81).

ESPECIALLY *for* YOU

The nicer the place, the more you should consider ordering one of the specials. While the specials in seedier venues often involve food that the kitchen is trying to get rid of, the ones in finer establishments tend to be dishes that the chef spent extra time preparing and often contain the freshest ingredients.

DO NOT DISTURB: No matter what the formality of the restaurant, you should be considerate of those around you. Shouting, smoking, making bodily noises, talking/texting on your mobile, and engaging in any other disruptive actions should be avoided. Such activities will only garner negative attention.

FOODIE FAUX PAS: Even if your food is so beautifully presented it almost looks too good to eat, take a moment to assess your surroundings and your tablemates before snapping any food porn pics. The act of pulling out your mobile device can distract from the ambiance of the meal. Do so with caution.

TABLE TALK: A beautiful restaurant with delicious food is only part of a lovely dinner. Be sure to arrive at the table with some engaging conversation. Books, movies, interests, hobbies, vacations, and topical trivia all make great conversation starters.

KID CLUB: If you have children, take them only to places where they'll be welcomed. If the venue has a children's menu or crayons at the table, you are in the right place. A four-star restaurant after junior's bedtime is no fun for him, you, the waitstaff, or other patrons. If you take junior out and he acts up, you must say your good-byes.

GARÇON! In the movies, it is common to see someone signal a waiter by snapping his fingers in the air while calling out. This type of commotion will certainly draw attention to you, but not in a good way. It is much better to make eye contact with your server to beckon him to your table. Or, if your waiter is terribly busy and you can't get his attention, ask another server to let your waiter know you need him. As a last resort, you may excuse yourself from the table to find the manager or maître d' and communicate your need for your waiter.

NOT YOUR JOB: The members of the waitstaff work hard for their tips, so please let them earn their keep. Do not brush crumbs, stack plates, or pass glasses. You may think you are helping, but your movements can interfere with the flow of their work. Unless your server or busboy has specifically asked you to pass something, refrain from any such action.

FLIRTING FORBIDDEN: Yes, your waitress may be a twenty-year-old knockout who bats her eyes at you, but rest assured, she's only looking for a bigger tip. If you're on a date, your companion may not find your flirting with the waitress to be as harmless as you do.

FRIENDS AND FINANCES: You may be doing really well at work, but be aware of your tablemates' situations. Not everyone can afford to order the most expensive meal on the menu, let alone help pay for you to do so. For a shared check, be sure to have cash on hand and put in money for what you ordered, as well as your share of the tax and tip. Or ask for separate checks at the start of the meal when you place your orders.

DOWN THE MIDDLE: There are times when you're dining out with those in basically the same financial situation as yourself, and you split the bill down the middle. In this instance, you may ask your server to divide the bill in two and put an equal amount on each credit card. To ensure that all remains even, ask the other signer how much he plans to tip. You may match the other party's tip, or if you feel it is a bit low, make yours a few dollars more to ensure that the waitstaff isn't shorted.

ALWAYS THE HOST: When you are hosting a meal at a restaurant, call ahead or arrive before your guests to review the menu and your table. You should also indicate whether or not you want alcohol to be served. Before your party arrives, let the maître d' know that you don't want the bill to come to the table. Some establishments will ask that you leave a credit card at the beginning, while others are comfortable waiting until the end of the meal. Explain that after your guests are finished, you will walk them to the door and then return to settle the bill. Some of the finer restaurants will simply run your card and then mail you the receipt.

TO TIP OR NOT TO TIP: People are often surprised to hear that you are not obligated to leave a gratuity when the service is poor. However, while you're not required to tip in such a situation, you're also not allowed to leave nothing and just walk out of the restaurant. If the service was bad enough for you to even consider leaving without giving a tip, you need to speak with the manager so that she is aware of the problem and can talk to the server about modifying his behavior. Gentlemen never post nasty comments online and when disappointed, instead they allow the management the opportunity to correct the issue.

FORGET FIDO: As much as your puppy may love to eat your leftovers, think twice before asking for a doggie bag. When you're on a date, dining with business associates or clients, or eating at an upscale restaurant, it's best to leave the food there. If you are a struggling student out with family or close friends, then by all means, take the rest of your meal home.

COAT COLLECTION: If you're dining socially with a woman, at the end of the meal when it's time to leave, you should assist her with her coat. Stand behind her, hold the garment open from the collar, allow her to slip her arms into the sleeves, and then lift the coat so that it rests squarely on her shoulders. She will button, clasp, or zip the coat herself.

PATRONIZING
the
FINE ARTS

ATMOSPHERE & ATTIRE: So you bought a tuxedo to wear to your cousin's wedding and it's been sitting in your closet ever since. Going to the theater provides a great opportunity to get some use out of it! And what a wonderful way to impress a date. If you don't own a tux, not to worry—you don't need one for this type of occasion. But you should dress up a bit. A suit or at least a jacket and tie will show that you understand the unstated rules of the theater.

TIMING YOUR ENTRANCE: While you may take your seat at any time at arena football, this is not the case at a fine arts performance. So as not to disturb the performers and other audience members, arrive at least twenty minutes before the curtain is scheduled to go up so that you're settled before the show begins. In many instances, ushers will not let you take your seat after the performance has started until there is some sort of break, so unless you want to spend the first act waiting in the lobby, arrive ahead of time.

SPATIAL RELATIONS: For everyone to be comfortable at a performance, it is critical that each individual be considerate of personal space. Everyone is entitled to one armrest—there should be no wrestling for territory. Don't kick the seat in front of you, don't let your belongings infringe upon the space of others, and don't bring in noisy or smelly snacks.

LET THEM PASS: When others need to get into or out of your row, stand rather than simply pulling in your legs, as the former approach creates more space for maneuvering. If the area is especially cramped, consider stepping out of the row into the aisle to allow the others to pass; you may then return to your seat.

MAKING YOUR WAY: When you need to pass others in your row on the way to your seat, allow them time to rise or move out of the space. Be sure to say "please," "excuse me," and "thank you" as you face forward and scoot sideways toward your seat.

OFF TO THE OPERA

Many find the opera to be an intimidating (or boring) experience, but becoming acquainted with the story and music ahead of time can help you better enjoy the performance. If you don't get a chance to do a little research beforehand, be sure to read the program, which often provides a brief synopsis of the tale, as well as bios of the performers. Nowadays, some opera houses offer translation screens so you're not left wondering what that large lady is singing about. (Note that these screens come in handy even when the opera is in English.) Last but not least, if you're not sitting up front, you might want to bring opera glasses (these can also be rented at many opera houses).

SILENCE IS A VIRTUE: During a performance at the theater, opera, ballet, or other similar setting, the only sounds should be coming from the stage; this means that you are not allowed to talk while the singers, dancers, or actors are performing. This also means that the ringer on your cell phone should be off (even vibrate can be dangerous when next to keys, change, or a tin of mints).

THE ENJOYMENT OF OTHERS: As in any public venue, don't engage in any conduct that might disturb those around you. Wearing a ten-gallon hat, talking to your companion during the show, clearing your throat constantly, fidgeting, cracking your knuckles, illuminating the screen on your mobile, snapping gum (which you shouldn't be chewing in public anyway), sniffling, coughing excessively, and getting up and down from your seat are just some of the actions that are likely to detract from the main event.

OUTTA HERE: Do your best to remain in your seat during the show. If you need to get up and absolutely can't wait until intermission or the end of the performance, take the shortest way out possible. When you wish to return, try to wait for a break in the action so that you don't annoy the others in your row. (To help avoid the need to get up, make a pit stop in the restroom when you first arrive.)

ROCK CONCERTS

TUCK AWAY THE TUX: When you are going to a rock concert, casual clothing is, of course, appropriate. As always, though, your attire should be clean, unwrinkled, stain-free and completely cover your privates while leaving something to the imagination.

BEGIN BOOGYING: Dancing can be a wonderful form of expression, and performers like to know that their music inspires the audience to move. However, don't get so lost in the moment that you lose track of your body parts; accidentally hitting the person next to you is simply not acceptable. As in other entertainment venues, consideration of others is a priority.

FOLLOW THEIR LEAD: If all the fans are on their feet and dancing, you should be too. If everyone else has taken their seats and you're swinging from the rafters, it's time to tone it down.

SPORTING EVENTS

BOYHOOD BONDING: Starting at a young age, conversations among males often turn to the topic of sports. If you're a big fan, this passion certainly makes it easy for you to have light discussions with people you don't know. Simply recalling a great season, a jaw-dropping upset, or a record-breaking event will generate enough information to make it through almost any conversation.

ONLY A GAME: Just because you're a guy doesn't mean you're required to love sports—it is, of course, fine if you don't. But even if sports aren't your thing, you should regularly check out the home page of sports websites so that you aren't totally lost if the topic comes up (at a minimum, you should know what sporting season it is and what local team is playing).

HOSTILE TERRITORY: Your team may very well be the best—or that may just be your opinion. Either way, be conscious of where you express your point of view. Crowds are notoriously unpredictable. If you're at a game and surrounded by fans from the other side, try to refrain from chanting a taunting cheer.

PERSONAL FOUL: There tend to be more incidents involving disorderly conduct at sporting events than at other happenings. The combination of testosterone and alcohol can be a dangerous one. As always, when out in public, keep your wits about you. Don't cross the line between being a fun-loving guy and being a liability.

PLACES *of* WORSHIP

SHOW RESPECT: When you enter a place of worship, it is critical that you demonstrate respect through both your attire and your attitude. Refrain from chewing gum, answering your cell phone (the ringer of which should be off), talking during the service, or engaging in any other activity that might be disturbing or offensive to others.

SUIT UP: If you are not familiar with the specific dress code, chances are you'll be safe wearing a dark suit, a white shirt, and a conservative tie. Religious symbols (other than those belonging to the house of worship's faith) should be hidden or extremely discreet.

HEADS UP: When entering a place of worship, look around to see if the other men have their heads covered or not. You should follow in kind. (When head coverings are required, they are made available to worshipers in an area outside the entrance to the actual sanctuary.)

ASK AHEAD: If you're attending a service with which you're unfamiliar, ask those who have invited you what to expect. You should inquire about the type of service, the length of the service, and any rituals that will take place. You may also ask about the dress code. If you're uncomfortable or unable to ask anyone, search the Internet or visit your local library to obtain some basic background information so that you are prepared.

PARTICIPATION PROTOCOL: Out of respect, you should stand when the congregation stands and sit when the congregation sits. If you aren't comfortable bowing, kneeling, or prostrating yourself, when the congregation does so, simply remain seated (when others are kneeling, though, sit forward in the pew to give the person behind you ample space). You are not required to perform any religious rite that makes you feel uncomfortable in any way. If you have been asked to participate in a certain part of the service and you don't wish to do so, politely decline.

MONETARY MATTERS: Attitudes toward bringing up the issue of money during religious services vary as widely as the services themselves. The leaders of some houses of worship feel it is their duty to collect from the congregation when the members are gathered; others will make no mention of money during services. If a collection is taken, as a guest, you are not obligated to donate. However, if you have enjoyed the service or feel so moved, your contribution will, of course, be welcomed. You may donate on the spot with cash and often with a credit card, send a check later, or donate on line.

STAY OR GO: Religious services vary in length. For a service that is under an hour, you should make every effort to remain for the duration. When it comes to longer services, you should time your exit so that it does not interfere with the worshipers or the person conducting the service. Occasionally, there will be portions of a service when no one is allowed to enter or leave; usually ushers are stationed at the doors during these periods.

FUNERALS

DEEPEST CONDOLENCES: When you learn of someone's death, you should contact the family and friends of the deceased to express condolence; if you can do so in person, that is best. Otherwise, you should do so by telephone, lastly by written word (for information regarding condolence notes, see page 158). Reasonable attempts should be made to attend the funeral service as a showing of support to those in mourning.

PAUSE BEFORE POSTING: Wait for an official online memory book or website before posting condolences as it would be cruel for loved ones to learn of the death via social media instead of a relative or friend.

SPREAD THE WORD: As unpleasant as it may seem, unless the family has specifically asked otherwise, once you learn of someone's death, you should contact anyone else you feel may need this information. Consumed with their loss and the funeral preparations, most mourners don't have time to call everyone. Furthermore, the mourners may not know all of the deceased's acquaintances. "Sad News" is the usual subject line for e-mail.

SAYING GOOD-BYE: The ceremonies with which we mark the end of someone's life are as varied as the ways we live. Some feature the deceased's favorite music as a celebration of life; others revolve around prayer and focus on death as a somber passing. If you'll be attending a funeral and you're unfamiliar with the particular religion, find out in advance what will occur. When you are especially close to the mourners, you may ask them directly. Other avenues of research include the funeral home, the house of worship, and the Internet.

SAY SOMETHING: Many people fear that they will say the wrong thing to those in mourning—so much so that they say nothing. Those who are grieving need to hear that you care. Typical expressions of condolence include "I am so sorry to learn of your loss" and "You and your family are in my thoughts and prayers."

SEND SOMETHING: To express sympathy, it is common to send something to the bereaved. The typical offerings are flowers and food. For followers of Buddhism and Hinduism, only flowers are given. In Judaism, it is common that food be brought to the family. Both flowers and food are acceptable in Christianity and Islam.

DONATIONS: In almost every situation, those in mourning will appreciate donations to charities, which may be made in memory of the deceased instead of giving food or flowers. Often, mourners will include in the obituary the names of suggested charities for those who would like to make a contribution. If individual charities have not been specified, consider the deceased's likes and activities when choosing an organization.

ATTIRE: For most faiths, attire at a funeral is conservative and somber. You'll most likely be safe with a dark suit, a white shirt, and a somber tie.

BEFORE AND AFTER: Members of some religions include other rituals in addition to the funeral to mark a person's passing. For instance, Catholics sometimes have a wake (typically a day or two before the funeral) for people to pay their respects. Family members and close friends will attend the burial; most mourners do not expect other funeral attendees to witness the burial. Many do expect funeral attendees to pay their respects at a private home after the burial. Generally, those conducting the funeral service will provide information about the burial and condolence calls. Many Jewish people sit shivah at home for a week after the funeral; this is a time to remember the deceased and offer condolences to the mourners.

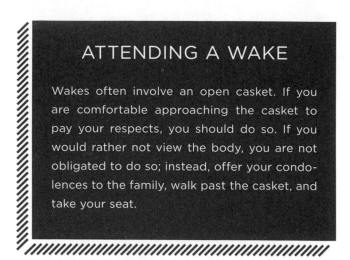

ATTENDING A WAKE

Wakes often involve an open casket. If you are comfortable approaching the casket to pay your respects, you should do so. If you would rather not view the body, you are not obligated to do so; instead, offer your condolences to the family, walk past the casket, and take your seat.

THE YEAR TO COME: For many people who have lost loved ones, the whirlwind surrounding the funeral is all-consuming. Often, it is only in the subsequent weeks and months that the feeling of loss really hits. Be sure to call, visit, and write the bereaved in the long days that follow, especially around holidays and birthdays.

REMOVED RESOURCES: If a member of your community has passed and you were not close to the individual or the family, you may not feel comfortable attending the funeral. But you can still provide support and assistance. If you are a neighbor, you can offer to watch the house while the funeral is taking place, or even help to prepare and set up the food to be served afterward. If the funeral is out of town, you can volunteer to pick up the mail or walk the dog.

from CLUELESS *to* CLASS ACT

CHAPTER TWO

The GENTLEMANLY GUEST

THE SMOOTH AND SOPHISTICATED MAN would not be caught dead arriving at a friend's home for a dinner party or a weekend stay empty-handed. He knows that when he is invited to someone else's home, his responsibilities extend beyond simply showing up. Don't worry—as a guest, you still have it easier than the host (though, as you will see in the next chapter, once you've been invited somewhere, you'll eventually need to reciprocate).

GENERAL GUIDELINES

RSVP: Whether an invitation has been extended via mail, telephone, or electronically, it is your responsibility to respond "yea" or "nay" promptly so that the host can plan accordingly. Do not put the host in the position of needing to hunt you down.

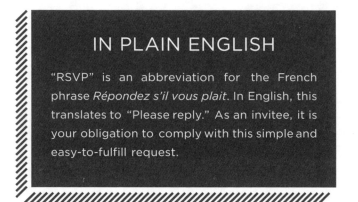

IN PLAIN ENGLISH

"RSVP" is an abbreviation for the French phrase *Répondez s'il vous plait*. In English, this translates to "Please reply." As an invitee, it is your obligation to comply with this simple and easy-to-fulfill request.

BE UP-FRONT: If you have any dietary restrictions (whether based on religious beliefs, philosophical ideology, or health needs), let your host know when you respond to the invite. (It is then up to the host to decide whether or not to accommodate you.) Do not treat your host like a short-order cook.

NO EXTRAS: Unless your host has specifically said you should feel free to bring other people to the get-together, only those on the invitation are invited. You may be dying to bring the latest love of your life, but refrain from asking the

from CLUELESS *to* CLASS ACT

host if you may do so, as this will only put him in an awkward position. If you really want to introduce this new paramour to all of your friends, throw your own party.

ADULTS ONLY: If you have kids and they weren't included on the invitation, don't bring them to the event.

FURRY FRIENDS FORBIDDEN: Unless your pets were specifically invited to the gathering, they are not permitted to attend. While a casual barbecue might seem like a great place for your new puppy to run around, your host might not share your opinion.

PITCHING IN: It is always a nice gesture to ask the host if there is anything you can do or bring. Be prepared to follow through if the host accepts. If the host declines, don't push it.

DON'T GO EMPTY-HANDED: When you go to someone's home for a party, you should bring a gift. Some appropriate options include wine or chocolates. If you plan to give flowers, it is best to send them in advance (along with a note of anticipation) so that they arrive the morning of the event; that way the host doesn't need to drop everything in order to find a vase in the middle of the festivities.

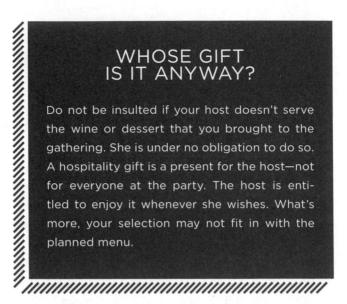

WHOSE GIFT IS IT ANYWAY?

Do not be insulted if your host doesn't serve the wine or dessert that you brought to the gathering. She is under no obligation to do so. A hospitality gift is a present for the host—not for everyone at the party. The host is entitled to enjoy it whenever she wishes. What's more, your selection may not fit in with the planned menu.

PICK A PART: For people who aren't terribly outgoing, attending a gathering can be a daunting prospect. If you tend to be introverted, offer to assist the host. Tasks such as taking people's coats and serving drinks allow you to interact with other guests in a nonintimidating way.

ACCIDENTS HAPPEN: If you break something in someone else's home (or clog the toilet), inform the host immediately. Say you're sorry, volunteer to help clean up, and offer to replace the item. (The host should graciously accept your apology and refuse your offer to supply a replacement.) Once you have taken these steps, do not dwell on the incident at the event (doing so will only put a damper on the festivities). However, once you are back at home, you should send a note of apology and a small gift.

TOILET TRAINING: When living alone or with a bunch of guys, you're free to leave the toilet seat in whatever position you desire. However, if you're a guest in someone's home, take a moment between the time you flush and wash your hands to put the seat down. (While we're on the subject, you should also take this step if you're having company at your own place or cohabiting with the fairer sex.) If you're in a home with small children or pets, you should lower the lid as well.

GO WITH THE FLOW: If you're attending a dinner party, eat dinner. If you're at a dance, get up and dance. If you're going to a costume party, wear a costume. Refusing to comply with the program will only attract negative attention.

PARTY PROTOCOL

WHAT TO WEAR: It used to be that a tuxedo, a suit, or khakis and a button-down shirt were the clothing options when going out. But men's dress codes have blurred and morphed so much over the past few years that it's hard to know what to wear anymore. If you're uncertain about what's appropriate for a certain event, when you call to RSVP, ask the host. When in doubt, it's better to be overdressed than underdressed.

ENTERING ON CUE: For most meal-related events, you should arrive within minutes of the time stated on the invitation. For free-flowing affairs, such as a cocktail party or housewarming, make your entrance when you anticipate the party to be in full swing. The exact timing varies depending upon social circle and geographic region, among other factors. Get acquainted with the social norms that apply to your particular situation, and plan your timing accordingly. If you really want to play it safe, arrange to meet up with a few people prior to the event so that you don't find yourself walking in alone.

DO YOUR PART: While the host should make sure all of the guests are having fun, the guests need to entertain themselves and others. Be sure to have some interesting—but not contentious—topics to discuss with others. (For information on carrying on a conversation, see the section that begins on page 111.)

EXPAND YOUR CIRCLE: Sure, parties are great places to catch up with friends, but take advantage of these opportunities to expand your social circle. You never know, you may find a new roommate, meet a promising business contact, or become acquainted with a potential romantic partner.

TIMING YOUR EXIT: At dinner parties and most other meal-related events, you are free to leave after most guests have finished eating dessert. When attending cocktail parties and the like, you should say your good-byes when the room starts to clear.

HASTA LA VISTA: One sure sign that you've overstayed your welcome is that the cleanup has begun. If you're a close friend of the host, by all means stay and help. Otherwise, you should be long gone.

THANKS A MILLION: When leaving a party or another type of gathering, take the time to find and thank the host. Let this person know what a wonderful time you had. Parties are a lot of work, and a little recognition will go a long way.

STAYING OVER

TALK, TALK, TALK: Clear and honest communication is the key to a successful visit. Well in advance of your arrival, you should make sure that the length of your stay and your specific arrival and departure times are convenient for your host. Also, ask whether there's anything you should bring from home (towels or sheets, for instance) that will help to make your stay easier.

CHAUFFEUR WANTED: Your host may not be able to drop everything to pick you up from the airport or train station, take you back when it's time to leave, or drive you around town—nor is he obligated to do so. He's not running a limo service, after all. If he offers, by all means, accept; otherwise, you'll need to take care of your own transportation.

BE THE BEARER OF GIFTS: Do not arrive empty-handed. The longer the stay, the more lavish the present. Wine, chocolates, baked goods, coffee table books, decorative items for the house, and kitchen gadgets all make for fine hospitality gifts. When traveling from out of town, a little something from your point of origin can be a special touch.

THIS ISN'T A HOTEL: Make yourself useful by helping around the house; clear dishes, offer to pick up something at the store, or (if the host is agreeable) make dinner. Do not expect the host to wait on you hand and foot. If that's what you wanted, you should have booked a hotel room. In addition to pitching in with some of the daily chores, if you're staying for more than two nights, you should take the host out for a nice meal (even if your visit is short, you may want to consider this gentlemanly gesture, though it's not a requirement).

KEEP IT CLEAN: Always pick up after yourself when you're a guest in someone's home. Make your bed, keep the bathroom and room that you're sleeping in tidy, hang up wet towels, and don't let your personal belongings take over the place.

PRIVACY, PLEASE: While your host may be absolutely thrilled to have you around, you should give him a break every now and then. Everyone needs a little space from time to time. Try to stay out from underfoot. Take a nap, read a book, or go for a long walk. Even better, take a day to see the sights. Invite your host, but be sure to give him the opportunity to decline. "I am off to see the Empire State Building today. If you would like to join me, you are more than welcome, but please don't change your plans on my account. I know how busy you are right now."

IN SYNC: Do what you can to mirror the schedule of the household. Your bedtime and wake-up time should be adjusted to match your host's. This is especially important if you are sleeping in a common room.

PERMISSION REQUIRED: Whether you wish to watch television, have a snack, or take an aspirin from the medicine cabinet, don't do anything or use anything belonging to your host without asking first. Being a guest in someone's home does not automatically grant you access to everything in the closets and cupboards.

THE MAGIC WORDS: Saying "please" and "thank you" is especially important when staying in close quarters. And don't forget "excuse me."

FAIR SHARE: Even if you're visiting family, once you've stayed longer than a few days, you should offer to contribute to the grocery bill. Most hosts will decline, but the offer is important.

SPEAK UP: If you have finished an item, be sure to mention it to the host. And if possible, make yourself useful in the process. For instance, you might say something like, "Sam, if you tell me where you keep the toilet paper, I would be happy to replace the empty roll in the upstairs bathroom."

FINAL FAREWELL: At the end of your stay, check around the house for any wayward personal items, tidy the room you were occupying, and attempt to empty the wastepaper basket. You must also strip the bed. Loosely fold the sheets, and leave them on the floor or bring them to the laundry area. The blanket and comforter should be folded neatly and placed at the foot of the bed.

CAN'T THANK YOU ENOUGH: You may have already thanked your host profusely in person, but don't stop there. Send a written thank-you note once you have returned home. Remember, a gracious guest is a welcome guest.

WEDDINGS

BY INVITATION ONLY: Unless the invitation specifically states "and guest" or "and family," you can presume that only the people specifically named on the invitation are invited. While you may think that others should be invited, the decision is not yours. If you have recently gotten married or engaged and your significant other was not invited, you may of course communicate your change in status and request that she be added to the list. Otherwise, do not ask to bring someone. For you singles out there, weddings are great places to meet potential significant others!

WHAT TO GIVE: The vast majority of engaged couples register for items they would like to receive. Today's brides and grooms not only "sign up" for such traditional gifts as china, flatware, crystal, kitchen items, linens, and decorative household objects, but also major appliances, electronics, entertainment equipment, and even contributions to the honeymoon or a new home. While you're sure to make the couple happy with a present from the wish list, you don't need to restrict yourself to the registry. Often, the most cherished and personal wedding gifts are those selected with special thought.

WHAT TO SPEND: Many people wonder how much money should be spent on a wedding gift. The answer varies according to many factors. First and foremost, you should consider your budget (not what is being spent by the wedding host). Then you should consider your relationship with the couple getting married. Amounts vary widely based upon geographic regions and the customs of your social circle.

from CLUELESS *to* CLASS ACT

PAY FOR POSTAGE: Whenever possible, send the wedding present in advance to the couple at home instead of bringing it to the event, as gifts (and checks) are easily misplaced during the festivities. If you can, put the card for the gift inside the package or wrapping so that it doesn't get lost.

DELIVERY DEADLINE: Someone somewhere began a rumor that a guest may wait up to one year to give the wedding couple a gift. This is simply not an acceptable practice. Ideally, gifts should be given before the wedding.

TO GIVE OR NOT TO GIVE: The question often arises as to whether or not an invitation to a wedding carries with it a gift requirement if you don't attend. The answer is that wedding announcements and wedding invitations do not carry any such obligation. That said, I do recommend sending a card with your well wishes when you receive a wedding announcement, and at least a small gift if you have been invited to the wedding. But certainly you know your relationship with the bride and groom much better than I, and you will need to make the call as to what action is most appropriate. Invitations are not invoices.

TO TUX OR NOT TO TUX: Guys are lucky in that their attire for a wedding is pretty much spelled out for them. If the invitation says "black tie," you should don a tuxedo, whether you own one or need to rent. When an invitation says "black tie optional," you should wear a tuxedo if you own one. In this situation, if you don't own one but are close to the bride and groom, you should rent one—otherwise you are off the hook and may wear a suit. For daytime weddings, a suit and tie are appropriate. For a beachside wedding or a daytime wedding in the summer or a tropical climate, a seersucker suit may be worn. If a wedding is so casual that a suit is not required, there is usually some instruction on the invitation; for instance, an invite to a scuba wedding—where the couple is literally taking the plunge—might say "Wear your swim trunks."

CEREMONY AND CELEBRATION: If you've been invited to both the marriage ceremony and reception, you may not go to the latter without attending the former; the ceremony is not optional. Skipping the ceremony and going only to the party is extremely tacky behavior.

ARRIVE BEFORE THE BRIDE: This advice may seem obvious, but for some reason, there are always stragglers. Make every effort to arrive at the wedding ceremony prior to the bride's stroll down the aisle. Most guests arrive twenty to thirty minutes before the time indicated on the invitation. When deciding when to leave your home or hotel for the ceremony, account for traffic and possible parking issues—and then add a little extra time to be safe. Arriving late can distract the happy couple as well as other guests.

LEAD THE WAY: A properly trained usher will greet you at the door to the wedding. If you're attending the event with a date, she will take the usher's arm to be escorted to the seating; you should follow behind. If you are attending solo, you would simply walk next to the usher (there's no need for you to take his arm).

PHOTO SHOOT: As long as you have not been informed that the ceremony site prohibits photography, pictures may be taken during the processional and recessional—but that's it. At all other times during the ceremony, the only person allowed to be clicking away is the photographer hired for the event. The clicks and flashes can be highly distracting and, in some instances, be viewed as disrespectful.

COUPLES' CHOICE: Even if it is not a Hollywood wedding, those who are being married may decide if they want their guests to post pictures during the event. Some couples create their own hashtag and believe the more uploads, the more blessings. Other couples prefer privacy. Respect their wishes.

HANDS FREE: No matter how late the night or how dehydrating your morning run, you should chug your coffee or juice so that you enter the service empty-handed. And after the processional photo, your mobile device goes away until the service is over.

DON'T BE A CRITIC: Weddings tend to be long functions, and you may exhaust your typical topics of discussion. However, you should not resort to making disparaging remarks about the bride, the groom, or the event. If you find the conversation at your table beginning to lag, this might be a good time to get up and dance.

SWEET ENDINGS: Hopefully you are able to relax and enjoy the wedding festivities. If you have accepted the reception invitation, you should remain at the party until the wedding cake has been cut. Once this ritual has taken place, you may leave if you must.

GRACIOUS GOOD-BYES: Before you leave, be sure to wish the wedding couple well, congratulate the families of the bride and groom, and thank the wedding hosts (i.e., those listed on the invitation).

LOST IN SPACE: If you have not received an acknowledgment that your wedding gift was received within six weeks of the wedding, you should take action. Call the couple, and say that you just wanted to make sure that your gift had arrived since you would be terribly upset if it had gotten lost in the mail and they thought you had not sent anything. If it turns out that the present was not received, call the store to track it down. If the gift was received, it is up to the couple to thank you during the conversation and to write you a note expressing their appreciation immediately.

//

CHAPTER THREE

The HOSPITABLE HOST

\\

NOW THAT YOU KNOW HOW TO BE THE perfect guest, it is time to examine what you need to do to be the perfect host. Relationships entail a certain amount of reciprocity. Yes, as a good guest you brought a gift for the host, but your obligations don't end there. Once you have been invited somewhere, you must ultimately return the invitation; this means you must become a host yourself. Do not panic. Being a host is not as difficult as you might think. And you can tailor your gathering to suit your entertaining capabilities and comfort level.

The ART *of*
ENTERTAINING

KNOW YOUR LIMITS: The first step in planning a party or other get-together is to figure out your budget—this factor alone will have a tremendous effect on your guest list, menu, and activities. Be realistic. You should never go into debt planning a party. (Keep in mind that there are always a few unexpected expenses, so give yourself a little cushion up front.)

YOUR GRACIOUS GUESTS: Your guest list should begin with those people to whom you owe invitations. Then you need to consider the personalities of your prospective guests to decide who else should be invited (and to what event). If this is the only party you are having this decade, your guest list will be long. If you entertain more often, you'll be better able to pick and choose the specific mix of people at each event.

SMALL STEPS: If you're a first-time host, it's best to start off with a relatively small and simple gathering. A pasta dinner for four, for instance, might not be too daunting. As you become more comfortable entertaining, you can plan bigger events.

PLAY TO YOUR STRENGTHS: Are you a gourmet chef? Then prepare a fabulous meal for your guests. Are you a movie buff? Have a group of friends over for a showing of your favorite flick (complete with a variety of gourmet popcorn and other snacks). If you're a microbrew connoisseur, invite guests for a tasting. If you're a restaurant aficionado, treat some friends to a meal at an establishment (not fast food) that you enjoy (while this can be an expensive endeavor, it is a great way for those who don't cook or are intimidated by the thought of entertaining at home to fulfill their hosting obligations).

EASY ENTERTAINING

So you haven't had much—or any—experience being a host. Not to worry. There are plenty of low-maintenance ways of entertaining. Consider having a group of people over to watch a big sporting event on television. The game provides automatic entertainment. All you need to do is supply the food and drink. The hors d'oeuvres can be as simple as pretzels and chips and salsa (you might opt to throw in some veggies and dip as a healthier alternative), along with some beer and soda to wash everything down; then, for the main course, you could order pizza or a six-foot hero. If you'd like to have a dinner party but cooking isn't your thing—and catering isn't in your budget—order your favorite ethnic take-out food and serve it on your best dishes.

ALWAYS OFFER: Even when a friend stops by unexpectedly, a good host always offers something, so have more than tap water and ketchup packets on hand. A respectable pantry has some simple staples such as tea bags, honey, crackers, cookies, pasta, tomato sauce, and chocolate. A respectable fridge has cheese (unopened hard cheeses such as sharp cheddar can last for months at a time), juice or iced tea, and bottled water. And a respectable freezer has gourmet frozen pizza, ice cubes, ice cream, and coffee (the beans last longer in the freezer).

COMPANY'S COMING: If you have invited guests over, you'll need to feed them according to the time of day. Morning menus can be as simple as fruit, doughnuts, and coffee or as complex as a full-scale brunch with omelets, pancakes, and fruit smoothies. Midday menus can be as simple as tuna salad sandwiches or as complex as a lunch buffet. Afternoon menus can be as simple as veggies and dip or as complex as hot hors d'oeuvres. Evening menus can be as simple as pizza or as complex as a home-cooked gourmet meal. Before you do any inviting, think about what you are willing and able to serve when your guests arrive. Then plan accordingly.

DRINKS ALL AROUND: If you will be offering your guests alcoholic beverages, you must also provide nonalcoholic options, such as soda and sparkling water.

BAR BASICS: Just as you would plan the menu for your food, you should plan the menu for the bar. When hosting smaller parties, you can perform the role of bartender yourself. For larger parties, hire a bartender so that you have more time to interact with your guests. Limiting your alcoholic offerings to beer and wine is a perfectly acceptable step that will help make your job easier. If you want to include mixed drinks, consider offering only one or two signature drinks so that you don't need to spend the whole time creating concoctions for your guests (perhaps margaritas for a summer soirée, or gin and tonics for a pre-theater gathering). If you plan to play bartender, make sure you know what you're doing. At the very least, purchase a cocktail guide and a bar mixing set. Even better, sign up for an adult education bartending course!

GREAT GLASSES: If you live like the Great Gatsby and own a plethora of barware and stemware, wonderful. If not, attempt to acquire at least a set of tumblers and some all-purpose stemware. For those of you who aspire to the finer things, here are some glasses that you might want to have on hand.

BORDEAUX WINEGLASS: This red wineglass is large in size to allow for a greater amount of aeration (Bordeaux region wines need contact with the air). In addition, these wines have more sediment particles than others, and the larger glass allows these pieces to sink to the bottom.

BURGUNDY WINEGLASS: Boasting a balloon-shaped bowl, this red wineglass tends to be smaller than the Bordeaux. This is because Burgundy wines have less sediment and are formulated to be consumed without decantation or aeration.

WHITE WINEGLASS: This glass tends to be narrower at the lip than the stemware designed for red wine. The shape allows for the delicate bouquet to concentrate toward the top of the glass.

WATER GOBLET: As the name suggests, this piece of stemware is designed to hold water. Generally, it's slightly larger than the wineglasses.

CHAMPAGNE COUPE: Legend has it that this style of champagne glass was modeled after the breast of Helen of Troy and that the design was later updated by Marie Antoinette. Regardless of whether the stories are true, the design allows for the rapid loss of precious bubbles and is eschewed by champagne aficionados.

CHAMPAGNE FLUTE: This tall, thin glass is elegant with a purpose. The design allows for the bubbles to catch on the sides of the glass, roll down to the exact center of the bottom, and then rise, single file, to the surface. The better the design and the better the champagne, the better the behavior of the bubbles.

LIQUEUR: Smaller than a traditional wineglass, this piece of stemware is generally used to serve cordials and eaux-de-vie.

PILSNER: This tall, thin glass was designed for Pilsner beers to help accentuate the color and taste that distinguish them from other types of beer. Today, most people use this glass to serve any kind of beer.

BORDEAUX

BURGUNDY

WHITE WINE

WATER

CHAMPAGNE
COUPE

CHAMPAGNE
FLUTE

LIQUEUR

PILSNER

HIGHBALL

DOUBLE
OLD-
FASHIONED

MARTINI

BRANDY
SNIFTER

HIGHBALL: This tall, thin tumbler-style glass (i.e., sans stem) is used for cocktails mixed with either soda or water, as well as for soft drinks.

DOUBLE OLD-FASHIONED: Shorter and wider than the highball, this tumbler-style glass is used for drinks that contain only alcoholic ingredients; often, these drinks are served on the rocks.

MARTINI GLASS: This stylish glass is easily recognized by its slender stem, angular bowl, and wide rim. As its name suggests, this is the glass you would use to serve martinis.

BRANDY SNIFTER: Usually boasting a very short stem and a very round bowl, this glass is designed to be cupped in the palm of the hand. Brandy is best enjoyed warm, and the heat from the drinker's hand helps to warm the liquid.

INVITING GUESTS: Once you've started making plans for your gathering, you'll want to invite your guests. For more information regarding invitations, see pages 49–50.

A PLACE FOR PLASTIC: Match your plates to your party. When entertaining casually outdoors or in front of the television, you may use disposable plates, glasses, and utensils if you prefer to do so. (I would encourage you to avoid buying the cheapest ones, as they tend to fall apart.) However, if you're having a more sophisticated indoor gathering, forgo the plastic. A gourmet dinner party deserves your best china.

BEFORE AND AFTER: While it may be a hassle, you do need to clean your place before and after the event. That includes the bathroom (and be sure you have a few extra rolls of toilet paper on hand in an obvious place so guests can help themselves).

MOOD MUSIC: Like all other elements of a gathering, the music should match the mood. Unless you're having a dance party (or you've hired live entertainment), the music should be heard clearly only when everyone stops speaking. It is there to set a tone—not overwhelm the party. Use technology to your advantage. Create a playlist in advance of your favorite background tunes and then put it on shuffle so that you don't need to think about it.

TURN OFF THE TV: Unless you've invited people over specifically for the purpose of watching television—whether it's a football game or the latest episode of a favorite show—the television should be off when you have company.

COME ON IN: The way you greet your guests at the door helps to set the tone for your event. Plan to have as much of the prep work done in advance so that you are not crazed with last-minute details as the guests arrive. Welcome them, take their coats, offer them something to drink, and lead them to where the action is going to take place. If you are simply too busy, assign a close friend (or a shy one) to door duty.

BUDGET YOUR TIME

All of those "last-minute" things you need to do for a party add up quickly. Do as much in advance as possible, saving only those matters that can't be taken care of ahead of time for the day of the event; this means cleaning, shopping, and doing as much food preparation as possible beforehand. When budgeting your time, leave a little extra for each "to-do," as things have a way of taking longer than you expect—and there are always additional issues that come up. When planning your schedule for the day of, include an hour to get cleaned up and dressed. As people begin to arrive, you should be calm, collected, and ready to greet them at the door. Your attitude and behavior set the tone for the whole evening. If you're stressed and spending all your time in the kitchen, that uneasiness is likely to rub off onto your guests. However, if you're happy, centered, and attentive to the comfort of the group, the party is sure to be a success.

ROLLING ALONG: A good host knows how to keep the party moving. It is the host's responsibility to introduce guests to one another; in the course of doing so, the host should point out something the guests have in common in

from CLUELESS *to* CLASS ACT

an effort to lead them toward an interesting conversation (for more information on how to make an introduction, see page 112). It is also helpful to have some kind of activity planned, whether it's a trivia game, good old-fashioned charades, a rousing round of sing-along tunes led by yourself or a talented friend at the piano, great music for dancing, or even a make-your-own sundae bar. You know your guests better than anyone, so select some activity that you think they'll enjoy should the party need a little pick-me-up.

CHOOSE YOUR CUES: Just as you invited the guests to the party, it is up to you to bring the party to a close. A good host does not wait for the party to die a slow death. Actions such as formally thanking everyone for coming or turning off the music are major signals that the evening has come to an end. While you don't want to call it a night too soon, you should always leave your guests wanting more.

The PLEASURE *of* YOUR COMPANY

GETTING THE WORD OUT: After you've set your budget and started planning your menu, it's time to invite your guests. Invitations should reflect the tone of the event. If you're having a group over to watch the game or organizing a get-together at a pub after work, extending an invitation electronically or by text is just fine. For a more formal party, a mailed invitation is necessary.

THE WRITTEN WORD: When it comes to written invitations, there are a few different approaches. You may handwrite your invitations on stationery, purchase pre-printed versions that have blanks where you fill in the specifics of your event, or order customized invitations. There are varying degrees of formality for all three of these options. Note that the level of formality is expressed not only by the style of the invitation, but by the actual wording as well.

JUST THE FACTS: Invitations must provide guests with some basic information, including your name; the date, time, and location of the event; the type of gathering (birthday celebration, Mardi Gras bash, dinner party, cocktails, brunch, etc.); the date by which invitees should respond; and the contact information for responding. If the party is being held in someone's honor, that person's name should, naturally, be featured as well. A line regarding the expected attire may also be included.

TIMETABLE: For a casual gathering, you might extend the invitations the week before, but for a formal function, you might invite guests as early as months ahead of time. Telephone, text, social media and e-mail are generally used for casual events that are one to three weeks away. Mailed invitations are generally employed for events one to two months away. If your party involves out-of-town guests, you should extend the invitations well in advance (two months) to be sure that the folks who need to travel have time to make the necessary arrangements.

The DINNER PARTY

THE OPENING ACT: Dinner may be the main event at a dinner party, but it's not the only act. When your guests arrive, they should have some time to meet and mingle in the living room or some other gathering area before heading to the dinner table. And this mingling time should be accompanied by hors d'oeuvres and drinks. Appropriate offerings include anything from veggies and dip or cheese and crackers to warm passed hors d'oeuvres. (Budget minimalists might choose to put out a small bowl of mixed nuts and dried fruits instead.)

THE MAKINGS OF A MENU: When planning what to serve for dinner, keep in mind the following rule of thumb: the more unusual your entrée, the more common your side dishes. This approach helps ensure that even your less adventuresome guests will have something to eat.

HAPPY ENDINGS: Like a present that isn't wrapped (yes, you must wrap a gift before giving it), a dinner party is not complete without dessert. You can serve this much-anticipated course in the dining room, or you can mix things up a little and offer it in a more relaxed setting—the living room or, perhaps, the patio if you're fortunate enough to have one and the weather cooperates.

DINNER DECOR: A dinner party means dressing up—this goes for not only you and your guests, but the table as well.

All you really need are a few well-placed candles and a floral arrangement, though you can get more elaborate if you wish. Just make sure that your table adornments don't block guests' views of one another; you should also avoid blooms with strong scents, as these can interfere with your guests' enjoyment of the food.

SETTING THE STAGE: Well in advance of the dinner party, take a good look at all of the rooms in which you will be entertaining. Make sure that there are places for people to sit comfortably and rest their drinks (have plenty of coasters and cocktail napkins on hand). You might also want to remove any fragile or valuable items.

SPECIAL SEATING: When serving a sit-down meal, it is important to plot out your guests' positions at the table. If you are hosting a highly formal affair, there are specific rules to follow (see below). Otherwise, your primary goal should be to seat those with common interests near one another, as this will help spur conversation and promote a good time. Know that members of married and committed couples should not be seated next to each other (the reasoning behind this is that they've already heard the same stories a zillion times). The only exception to this rule lies with engaged people and newlyweds, who should be seated next to each other. When possible, many hosts alternate the seating by gender. However, this is a guideline, not a requirement. Be sure to seat any potential romantic interests side by side.

FORMAL FUNCTIONS: In formal situations, the following seating configuration is employed. The host sits at the head

from CLUELESS *to* CLASS ACT

of the table with the host's significant other at the foot. The guest of honor, if there is one, sits to the host's right. The guest of honor's significant other sits to the right of the host's significant other. The second most important guest is seated to the left of the host's significant other, while this important person's significant other is seated to the left of the host. The table is filled in this way based upon rank. Traditionally there is an even number of people, and whenever possible, the configuration would alternate between male and female.

CULTURAL VARIATIONS

Seating configurations vary according to culture. In many Asian cultures, the guest of honor is seated facing the door. In some Eastern European societies, the guest of honor sits at the middle of the table. Lastly, there are other cultures in which the guest of honor sits facing the most beautiful view of the room.

SEATING DESIGNATIONS: Your guests will look to you regarding where to sit. Setting out place cards ahead of time will take the pressure off you during the party and will result in less confusion for your guests when they gather at the table. If you don't take this step, you should be prepared to tell your guests where to sit as they approach the table.

SETTING
the TABLE

NEED-TO-USE BASIS: You should place on the table only dishes, utensils, and glasses that guests will actually be using during the meal. So if you're not serving a soup course, there is no need to include a soupspoon in the place settings.

CENTER STAGE: The plate belongs at the center of the place setting. When the entrée is being plated in the kitchen (as opposed to being served from platters at the table), there are three options. The first is to include the dinner plate in the initial setting, but then remove it when the time comes to serve the meal. The second is to put out a slightly larger plate, known as a charger, which is simply a placeholder (you would not eat food off this dish). The third is to leave the space where the plate will ultimately be placed empty at the start (this approach, however, makes the table seem a bit naked and is thus rarely employed for formal meals). The soup and salad dishes may be set upon the dinner plate or the charger when served.

FORKS: The forks are set to the left of the plate in the order that they will be used. The fork that will be used first should be farthest from the plate.

NAPKIN: In formal place settings, the napkin is generally placed to the left of the forks (this enables you to pick it up and put it on your lap without disrupting your flatware). In less formal situations, the napkin may be placed under the forks or on top of the plate. For safety's sake, you should never stuff a napkin in a water goblet.

KNIVES: With the exception of the butter knife, the knives belong to the right of the plate, arranged in the order that they will be used. The knife that will be employed first should be situated farthest from the plate. Make sure to set each knife so that the serrated edge faces the plate.

SOUPSPOON: If you are having soup, the soupspoon will be placed to the right of the knives.

DESSERT UTENSILS: When you include the dessert spoon and fork in your place setting from the start, these utensils may be situated directly above the plate in a horizontal position. The dessert spoon should be the uppermost utensil, with its handle to the right, and the dessert fork should be situated just below it, with the handle to the left.

BREAD PLATE: The bread plate should be situated above and slightly to the left of the forks. Place the butter knife (if you have enough for everyone) horizontally on top of the bread plate, with the handle to the right.

GLASSES: The glasses are placed above the knives and arranged so that they curve downward (see page 56 for their placement and order at a formal table). Were you to offer champagne as well, the champagne glass would be positioned farthest to the right with respect to the other glasses. (Please note that when the formal toasting doesn't take place until after the main course, the champagne glasses are not set, but rather filled and presented prior to dessert.)

For formal place settings, the coffee cup and saucer are not put out until dessert is served (at which point they would go above and to the right of the dessert plate). At a more casual meal, the coffee cup and saucer may be set at the beginning.

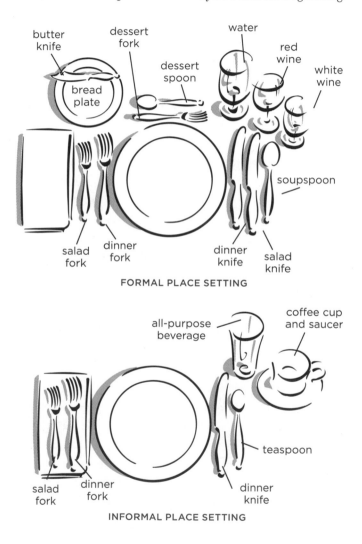

FORMAL PLACE SETTING

INFORMAL PLACE SETTING

from CLUELESS *to* CLASS ACT

OVERNIGHT VISITORS

BE CLEAR: When inviting someone to stay with you, be open about what you are and are not offering. Discuss logistics in advance, and then confirm the details a few days prior to the visit. Some topics that you'll want to cover include specific dates and times (both arrival and departure), travel arrangements (while you should give directions and advice, you are not required to provide transportation), where the guest will be staying within your home (especially if in a shared or common space, as opposed to a dedicated guest room), and anything your visitor should bring from home.

THE GUEST WING: Not every host has an extra bedroom for visitors—that's perfectly fine. The idea is to make your guest as comfortable as possible. Certainly your college roommate can get some shuteye on your pullout couch. Your grandmother, on the other hand, should be offered your bed, while you sleep on the pullout.

BATHROOM BASICS: You should provide your guest with a bath towel, a hand towel, and a washcloth, as well as a quick tutorial regarding any tricky fixtures. Also let him know what supplies he's welcome to use during his stay. Before your guest's arrival, you might want to audit your medicine cabinet for anything that should be hidden away. And, as you would when having guests over for a party, make sure that there are extra rolls of toilet paper on hand in an obvious place so your visitor doesn't get stuck in an awkward situation.

MINTS AND NICETIES: To be the best possible host, think about what you might want to have when staying somewhere else. Some welcoming items include:

- New (unused) travel-size shampoo, conditioner, lotion, and soap
- An extra toothbrush (in case your guest forgets to pack one), toothpaste, adhesive bandages, and headache relief—all in a spot readily accessible to your guest
- Reading materials
- A reading light, situated so that your guest can turn it on and off without getting out of bed
- A glass of water at bedtime—and a spot to rest it near the bed
- A waste basket
- An extra robe (clean, of course), which will certainly impress your guest

PANTRY PREP: You may be able to live on cold cereal and Gatorade®, but not all of your visitors will have the same diet. A week before a guest is due to arrive, ask what breakfast and snack foods he enjoys so that you can have some of his preferences on hand.

GROUND RULES: Any specific house rules should be discussed upon arrival. For instance, if you recycle, let your guest know where to discard newspapers or soda cans.

SHARING SPACE: If your guest will be sleeping in a common area, clear out a corner so that he can unpack his belongings. You should also make room in one of your closets for your guest's hanging items.

CARDS ON THE TABLE: Once your visitor has had a chance to settle in, talk about your schedules and the like. Any planned activities or events, typical mealtimes, and even what time everyone should be up the next day should be discussed. Both you and your guest are more likely to enjoy the visit if everyone knows what to expect.

BALANCING ACT: Having a guest in your home is going to alter your schedule. Some flexibility will, undoubtedly, be necessary. However, a vacation for your guest should not mean a ridiculous amount of labor for you. If your visitor is running you ragged, the next time he calls to visit, suggest a nearby hotel. That way you can both enjoy your time together.

LIGHT THE WAY: It is a good idea to put a night-light on in the hall or simply leave a hall light on in case your guest gets up in the middle of the night. In unfamiliar surroundings, a little illumination will be helpful and appreciated.

PET PROTOCOL

BEWARE OF FIDO: If you have a pet, when you invite people over, you should let them know. Some people have allergies, while others simply have a fear or dislike of certain furry or feathered creatures. In any case, guests shouldn't be caught off guard when they arrive.

CURB YOUR ENTHUSIASM: While you may enjoy greetings from your pet when you walk in the door, not all of your guests will want a sniff and a kiss. Try to contain your pet during the initial introductions. You may want to tucker out your pet ahead of time and then sequester him while you have company.

HAIRY SITUATION: If you're the proud pop of a pet, you'll need to go above and beyond when you've invited company. In addition to the typically cleaning, remove the pet hair from the surfaces where guests will be sitting. This means an extra pass over the couch with a vacuum. Since vacuuming tends to stir up dander, many pet owners do this a day in advance and then put a sheet over the sofa cushions to keep the surface fur-free until the guests arrive. (Plus, if you take care of this in advance, is it one less to-do item for the day guests arrive.)

HYGIENE HINTS: While your cat may regularly walk on your kitchen counters, don't allow her to do so when guests are over (especially if they're invited for dinner). You should also refrain from letting your dog lick your hand as you're making dinner. And no guest should have to endure a pet begging at the table.

//

CHAPTER FOUR

GRACIOUS DINING

\\

AH, THE ELEGANCE, THE ALLURE, THE intimidation of a well-set table. While everyone knows the etiquette police are not waiting to take you away if you use the wrong fork, many people are still filled with trepidation when dining at a social gathering. In this world of fast food, plastic utensils, and meals-in-a-mug, it is no wonder we are out of practice. The best way to be more at ease when dining out is to educate yourself. These guidelines are not difficult, and the more you know, the more comfortable you'll be—and the more you'll enjoy yourself.

UTENSIL USAGE
and
SILENT SIGNALS

DIFFERENCES IN STYLE: There are actually two different approaches when it comes to dining with forks and knives: American and Continental (although the latter term is technically a reference to Western Europe, the method can be found worldwide).

AMERICAN DINING: In the American style of dining, the tines face up once the food has been speared, and the fork is held in the right hand when transporting food from plate to mouth. When food needs to be cut, the fork is transferred to the left hand, tines down, and the cut is made with the knife in the right hand. Once the cut has been made, the knife is placed in the resting position on the plate (see illustration on page 64), and the fork is transferred back to the right hand.

CONTINENTAL DINING: In Continental dining, the fork is held in the left hand with the tines down, while the knife stays in the right. There is no switching of hands, and the knife is held between cuts rather than returned to the plate. The fork is turned toward the mouth (tines still down) using a twist of the wrist. Some consider Continental dining to be the "higher" method, because of the graceful motion of the fork and the relative quietness created by keeping the knife in one's hand as opposed to constantly placing it on the plate.

CONSISTENCY COUNTS: It doesn't matter whether you practice the American or Continental style of dining, as long as you pick one and stick with it throughout the entire meal.

OUTSIDE IN: Properly set utensils are placed in the order they will be used. Generally, you're safe to start with the utensils farthest from your plate, and then work your way in as you progress from course to course. If you are unsure, observe which utensil your host uses. Often, your dessert fork and spoon will be stationed above your plate (see the illustration of a formal place setting on page 56). If these utensils are not moved by your server when your entrée is cleared, you may bring the fork down to your left and the spoon down to your right.

CUTTING EDGE: Knives should be placed with the serrated edge facing your plate. The sharp edge faced out is seen as a sign of hostility toward your neighbor.

NEVER THE TWAIN SHALL MEET: Once a utensil has touched food, it must not touch the table's surface.

TAKING A BREATHER: By placing your utensils in the proper position, you send a silent message to your companions and any waitstaff, letting them know when you are simply resting and when you are finished with your meal. Think of your plate as the face of a clock. In both the American and Continental styles of dining, resting is indicated by placing the top of the knife at twelve o'clock and the base of the handle at four o'clock (with the serrated edge facing in, of course); meanwhile, the top of the fork should be placed at twelve o'clock and the base of its handle at eight o'clock. The only difference between the American and Continental resting positions is that the fork tines face upward in American dining but downward in Continental dining.

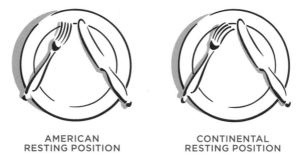

**AMERICAN
RESTING POSITION**

**CONTINENTAL
RESTING POSITION**

FINISHED: If you dine in the American style, to indicate that you are finished with your meal, situate the knife just as you would for resting, but place the fork (tines may be up or down) alongside the left edge of the knife. In Continental dining, you have a choice; you may either place the fork and knife as you would in the American style, or you may place the fork and knife so that they form an X.

**AMERICAN
FINISHED POSITION**

**CONTINENTAL
FINISHED POSITION**

SPOONING SOUP: When you eat soup, you move the utensil away from your body before bringing it to your mouth. Start by placing your soupspoon in the soup at the point that is closest to you and collect soup on the spoon as you move the utensil away from you; then, raise the spoon directly over the bowl and bring it to your mouth while keeping your back straight and leaning in slightly from your hips. Silently sip the soup (no slurping) from the side of the spoon. This should all be done in a single, fluid motion.

SOUP SUSPENSION: Because of the difference in the way it is served, soup has its own rules when it comes to utensil placement. When you are resting (as opposed to being finished), place the soupspoon in the cup or the bowl, with the handle at about three o'clock.

SOUP TO NUTS: When soup is served in a cup with a saucer, to indicate that you're done, put the spoon on the saucer behind the cup, with the bowl of the spoon to the left and the handle to the right. When the soup is in a bowl on a plate, if the rim of the plate is wide enough, place the spoon on the plate behind the bowl, with the bowl of the spoon to the left and the handle to the right. If the soup is in a bowl without a plate, or with a plate that is too small, the finished position is the same as resting, with the spoon inside the bowl.

**SOUPSPOON
RESTING POSITION**

**SOUPSPOON
FINISHED POSITION**

SALAD SCHEDULE: When you are dining in the American style, your salad will be served before the main course. In addition, at finer establishments, you will be provided with a salad knife (along with the usual salad fork) to help you cut the lettuce leaves into a manageable and polite bite size. In Continental dining, the salad is generally served after the entrée. Continental diners typically fold their salad leaves rather than cutting them.

DIG IN

SIMON SAYS: I liken gracious dining to a grown-up game of Simon Says. Your host is "Simon." Until this leader does—or tells you to do—something, you must wait. Simon is generally the person who did the inviting or the person who will be paying for the meal. If you are at someone's home, the home owner is Simon. If you are dining out at a restaurant, the person who coordinated the event is Simon. If you are with a group of friends at a restaurant and each of you will be covering your own costs, you are your own Simon, but you must watch what the other Simons at your table are doing.

MINE VS. YOURS: One of the biggest challenges when dining with others is figuring out which bread plate is yours and which water glass is yours. My favorite memory trigger is "B.M.W.," which in this instance stands for "Bread, Meal, and Water"; when you are sitting at your place setting, this is the order in which these items should appear from left to right (the same way you would read the letters).

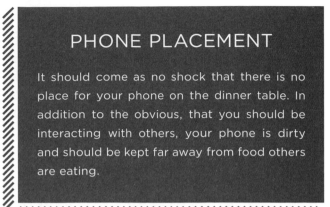

PHONE PLACEMENT

It should come as no shock that there is no place for your phone on the dinner table. In addition to the obvious, that you should be interacting with others, your phone is dirty and should be kept far away from food others are eating.

NAPKIN NOTICE: You should not take your napkin from your place setting until the host does so. When prompted, unfold your napkin completely, refold it in half, and place the fold at your knees with the other two corners at your hips. This allows you easy access to one corner at a time to wipe your mouth. If you are the host, or in a situation where there is no host, take your napkin from your place setting once everyone is seated comfortably.

FOOD TO FACE: Proper posture is an essential aspect of gracious dining. Sit with your back straight, leaning in slightly from your hips, and raise your food over your plate up to your mouth. Do not slouch or bring your face to your food.

ELBOWS OFF THE TABLE: In America, we rest our hands in our lap when we are not using them to eat. Just about everywhere else in the world, hands are kept at all times where everyone can see them.

SAME SETTINGS: Your place setting should match everyone else's, which means that you are not at liberty to rearrange it. While you may be tempted to bring your bread plate closer to you or move your water glass to your left, you must refrain from taking such action. The purpose of this arrangement is not merely to create an aesthetically pleasing table, but to enable other diners and the waitstaff to quickly and easily identify what belongs to you versus your neighbor.

EXCEPTIONS TO THE RULE

A great etiquette debate centers on plate rotation and adjustment. There are those who say that once a plate has been set, you may not move it at all. Others, myself included, allow for slight movements in certain situations to prevent an unfortunate occurrence. If the plate is precariously close to the edge, you are allowed one adjustment so that it doesn't end up crashing to the floor or falling in your lap. If the server set the plate so that the main portion of your entrée is farthest from you, making it difficult to cut, you are also allowed one adjustment.

from CLUELESS *to* CLASS ACT

GROUP GRATITUDE: You may find yourself in a situation where the host chooses to say a prayer before eating. If you don't feel comfortable praying, simply bow your head out of respect.

THE GREEN LIGHT: You should not begin eating until the host commences or signals you to do so (the only sustenance that may pass your lips before you have been given the go-ahead is water). The host may wait until everyone is served or—if the group is large or the course is hot—tell those who have food to start so that their meals don't get cold (the latter is the more gracious approach). If you start before everyone is served, eat slowly; you should still have food in front of you when the others receive their meals. When you are dining out in a situation where there is no host, you should wait until everyone has been served before digging in; and, in this situation, if you are one of the diners who doesn't yet have his dish, you may tell the others to go ahead and eat.

ROLL ROULETTE: The person sitting closest to the bread basket is the one who should set it off on its journey around the table. If you're at a gathering with a host, the host will give the signal as to when to start the bread; when dining without a host, you may start the bread after everyone has been seated, though I prefer to wait until everyone has ordered. If you find yourself closest to the bread, pick up the basket and while turning to your left, verbally offer a piece to the person sitting to your left (do not put your fingers on the bread itself). The recipient of your offer should then take a piece and put it on her bread plate while you continue to hold the basket. You may then take a piece for yourself and pass the basket to your right. Each person thereafter takes her own piece and continues passing to the right. Bread is the only item that is initially offered left and then passed right.

SMOOTH AS BUTTER: When you are taking some butter from a shared butter dish, put it on your bread plate—not directly on your bread. If you have your own butter knife, use it; otherwise, use the shared butter knife or fork accompanying the butter dish.

CRUMMY BEHAVIOR: The proper way to eat bread is not what people usually expect. Simply tear off a bite-size piece (see definition on below), place the rest of the bread back on your bread plate, butter only the piece that you are about to eat, and then pop it into your mouth. While this method does create a lot of crumbs, the result is expected and accepted.

BITE SIZE: When dining with others, you should take modest-size bites. The appropriate bite size is the amount of food you can chew three or four times and then swallow without choking. (Since you are forbidden to talk with your mouth full, taking relatively small bites will allow you to participate in the conversation more often.) The more important your company, the smaller your bite size should be. First dates and job interviews require smaller bites, whereas dinner with friends allows for a slightly larger bite.

SEE FOOD: Yes, this is an old elementary school joke, but while kids under the age of ten might find chewed food to be hilarious, adults don't. Chew with your mouth shut. If you are having trouble closing your mouth, revisit the definition of bite size.

COUNTERCLOCKWISE CIRCULATION: Platters and other serving dishes should travel around the table in a counterclockwise direction; in other words, pass to your right. In addition to preventing those Thanksgiving traffic jams that occur when food is being passed this way and that, the counterclockwise motion allows you to take the platter with your left hand, leaving your right hand free to serve. Since most people are right-handed, this permits the majority of people to serve themselves more easily, making mishaps less likely to occur. Lefties, hang in there; you win out during cocktail parties (see page 115).

TASTE TEST: Always taste your food before adding seasoning. You don't know how heavy-handed the chef is with spices, and the food may be flavorful enough already. Plus, if you're dining in someone's home, the person who prepared the meal may be insulted if you don't sample the cooking before trying to alter the taste.

MANNERS AND MOVING AHEAD

There is an apocryphal story about an executive who, when up for a promotion, was invited to lunch with the CEO. When the food came, the executive salted his food before tasting it. The CEO denied the promotion on the basis that the employee took action before gathering information to evaluate the situation.

CONDIMENTS THAT COMPLEMENT: While you should taste your food before adding salt or pepper to it, condiments may be added at any time, since this decision is usually based on personal preference as opposed to whether or not the food needs a little something extra. You already know if you like butter on your bread or sour cream on your baked potato or dressing on your salad.

SHARING SERVINGS: This practice should occur only with someone you know well. If you plan to split an order, let your waitperson know so that the food can be brought out on two separate plates, preventing you from needing to do the work—often a messy task—at the table.

COOL IT: If your soup is too hot to eat, allow it to sit and cool—do not blow on it. This is a good opportunity for you to converse with others.

CONCISE CUTTING: You should cut only the piece of food you are about to eat. This stems from practicality, preventing hot food from cooling down too quickly.

PURIST VS. MIXING: It is acceptable to take a bit of meat and a bit of vegetable on your fork and eat them in the same mouthful, as long as you don't overdo your polite bite size. However, mixing your entire meal on your plate may cause too much attention to be focused on you and your eating habits.

UFO'S AND "IFO'S": Unidentified flying objects and identified fallen objects should be handled with care. When you're at a restaurant, once a utensil hits the floor, it is no longer in your domain; you should signal a waitperson to bring you a new one. If you are at someone's home, pick up the utensil and take it into the kitchen to be washed before use. A gracious host will jump up to help you. If he is otherwise occupied or you're attending a casual gathering, you may wash the utensil yourself.

SPILLS AND THRILLS: For some, it is challenging to make it through a meal without spilling something or dropping a morsel of food. If a piece of lettuce falls from your plate onto the table or your lap, you should discreetly pick it up and put it back on your plate (not to be eaten). If it falls on the floor, let it be. If you knock over your wineglass, cover the spill with your napkin. At a restaurant, the waitstaff will take it from here. When you're in someone's home, ask the host what you can do. If she says you shouldn't do anything, allow her to clean the spot.

FAST FINISH: If you find that you always finish your meal before everyone else, it's time to slow down— you should be eating at the same pace as those around you. For those who tend to be the last ones finished, I would never recommend eating faster, as doing so is bad for digestion. However, you should come prepared with questions to ask others to ensure that the conversation keeps flowing as you finish your food.

THE CLEAN PLATE AWARD: Many people were admonished as children to finish everything on their plates. As adults, this is not always a necessary, or desirable, course of action. You should moderate your food intake according to where you are, the people you are with, and the number of courses that will be coming to the table.

GOOD TO THE LAST DROP

Another great etiquette debate involves whether or not to finish all of the food on your plate. There are those who say it is wasteful and insulting to your host if you don't eat everything. Others feel you must always leave a little something so that your host doesn't think you didn't have enough to feel satisfied. I tend to leave just a little on my plate. In situations where there are heaping bowls of mashed potatoes and an entire platter of turkey on the table, it is obvious that there is more than enough food to go around, so you should feel free to polish off everything on your plate.

TIME TO CLEAR: When you are a guest for a meal at someone's home, you may offer to help clear dishes between courses or at the end of the meal. However, if the host declines your offer, abide by this decision. Do not insist.

NO WHITE LIES: When served something you don't enjoy, do not call attention to yourself. Find the pieces you like and eat them; move the others around on your plate—you are not required to eat them. (Under no circumstances should you banish the unwanted food to your bread plate.) If someone draws attention to your picky behavior, simply laugh and

from CLUELESS *to* CLASS ACT

change the topic. Do not directly answer any question about why you're not eating something, as this could create more trouble. For instance, if you say that you're not hungry but then gobble down dessert, your tablemates will know you were lying. If you go into detail as to why you aren't eating, your host may try to remedy the problem, thereby drawing more attention to you and your food—and away from the company.

UNWANTED INTRUDERS: If there's a hair or bug in your food, you'll need to size up the situation before taking any action. If calling attention to the issue is going to disrupt your big lunch interview or make your first date even more awkward, it's better to just pick around the offender. If you're at a restaurant and you decide to call your server over, be sure to whisper the problem so as not to upset your tablemates. Making the others queasy is poor form. The same principle applies to dining in someone's home. Announcing that there's a hair in your food at your boss's dinner party is simply not a good idea.

IN AND OUT

There are differing opinions regarding the best way to remove something from your mouth that you'd rather not swallow. Some experts believe that substances should come out the same way they went in. Therefore, if you discover a piece of gristle in your mouth, since it went in on your fork, it should be spit onto your fork and transported to your plate. However, many etiquette consultants (myself included) find this approach to be unpleasant. Depending on your situation, you could swallow the gristle and chase it with a swift drink of water; excuse yourself from the table and spit it out in the bathroom; or carefully extract the offending piece from your mouth with your forefinger and thumb and place it on your plate so that it's hidden by your garnish. Spitting food into your napkin is not permitted.

STEMS, BONES, AND PITS: If a stem or a small bone makes its way into your mouth, clean it with your tongue, bring it to the front of your mouth, discreetly remove it with your forefinger and thumb, and place it on the edge of your plate. Watermelon seeds, cherry pits, and olive pits are usually spit into your closed fist.

NO BONES ABOUT IT: While you may derive extreme pleasure from gnawing the meat away from a bone, this is a habit that is best performed alone. Unless you are at an outdoor barbecue, you should eat only those pieces of meat you are able to obtain using your fork and knife.

QUICK CHECK: The period between the main course and dessert is an ideal time to excuse yourself to use the restroom and do a quick appearance check (you wouldn't want to spend the rest of the night with spinach stuck in your teeth). Don't linger, though. You should return to the table as quickly as possible so others do not need to wait for you in order to begin their desserts.

TEA TRASH: When you are served a pot of tea, the tea bag goes into the pot. When you are served a cup of hot water, the tea bag goes into the cup. Once the desired flavor has been attained, lift the tea bag out of the cup with the aid of your spoon. Keeping the bag on the spoon, twist the string once or twice around the bag to squeeze out the liquid. Then place the spoon with the tea bag behind your cup on the saucer.

TASTEFUL TOASTS: The best toasts are, in a word, brief. Toasts, which enhance the celebratory mood of an affair, can be given when everyone arrives at the table or just before dessert. Know that it is egotistical to drink a toast to yourself!

FOND FAREWELL: When the host stands to signal the end of the meal, you should stand as well. Unlike when you excuse yourself in the middle of a meal, you should place your napkin neatly on the table (as opposed to on your chair). Then, as always, exit from the right side of your chair, and push the seat of the chair under the table as you leave.

TABLE MANNERS

TABOO TOPICS: The topics of conversation that are not allowed at the dinner table include issues that could lead to a contentious debate and graphic descriptions of medical ailments or anything else that might make your companions queasy. The goal is for everyone to feel at ease to enjoy the conversation and the meal.

EXCUSE ME: If you need to leave the table for any reason, you should simply say, "Excuse me." No need to share your need for a restroom, craving for a cigarette, or desire to make a call. There is such a thing as too much information. After excusing yourself, stand up, place your napkin on your seat, push the seat of your chair underneath the table, and walk away.

CELL CONSTRAINTS: Only answer your mobile in case of serious emergency. On the rare occasion when you must respond, excuse yourself from the table to type a text or take a call.

OFF-LIMITS: Like cell phones, eyeglasses should never touch the top of the table. They do not belong on eating surfaces.

NO NOSE BLOWING: Do not blow your nose at the table. If your nose is a bit runny, you may dab it with your own tissue or handkerchief. Your napkin is not a tissue. When you need to blow your nose, you must excuse yourself from

from CLUELESS *to* CLASS ACT

the table and proceed to the restroom. Coughing should be done into your napkin and away from the table. If you are doing a good deal of coughing and nose blowing, there is a good chance you are too sick to be out with others. Go home.

A CAUTIONARY TALE

People often undervalue the importance of good table manners. But displaying poor table manners affects the way others perceive you. A corporate client once shared a story with me about how he had flown with a management team to another city to tell the executives of a small entrepreneurial company that they had won a four-million-dollar contract. When the team landed, they took the entrepreneurs out to dinner, where the CEO of the contracting company was so appalled by the entrepreneurs' table manners that he decided not to make the offer.

TEETH TROUBLE: If food is caught between your teeth, use the following three-step approach to dislodge it. First, close your mouth and run your tongue over your teeth to see if you can shake it free. (Make sure your tablemates aren't looking—they might think you're being suggestive!) Second, take a brisk drink of water. Third, if the stubborn offender is still in place, excuse yourself from the table and proceed to the restroom, where you may remove it. In North America, it is simply not acceptable to use your knife as a mirror while you pick at your teeth. And you are certainly not permitted to use your knife as a toothpick to clean your teeth. Should you decide to employ a toothpick in this endeavor, do so in the privacy of the restroom.

THE BROCCOLI DEBACLE: A fellow diner smiles at you, and you cannot help but notice the enormous piece of green caught between her two front teeth. What should you do? If you catch the person's eye and quickly point to your own teeth, she should pick up on the signal. If the other diners are caught up in conversation and you can whisper to this person without anyone noticing, do so. If you cannot get the point across discreetly, excuse yourself and on your way out whisper into her ear that she has something caught in her teeth. But, people ask, what if the person is an interviewer, a big client, or a first-time date? Won't calling attention to the problem make for an awkward situation? The answer is that you need to evaluate the situation based on the relationship and the person involved. Keep in mind, though, that the individual will most likely discover the problem at some point and suspect that you were aware of it, but held your tongue. The guideline here is "a small embarrassment now trumps a greater embarrassment later."

UP AND DOWN: In social settings, some women may still expect you to rise when they leave or approach the table. This practice originated because a gentleman would always help a woman in and out of her chair. Even if the lady is too fast for you, you should rise up a bit out of your chair as she leaves the table. When she returns, you should rise again to help her with her chair. If you have a VIP at your table, regardless of gender, the same respectful rise applies.

HANDLING YOUR LIQUOR

TO DRINK OR NOT TO DRINK: As mentioned in the restaurant section, you are not obligated to order an alcoholic beverage if others are doing so. However, you should order some type of refreshment, such as soda or sparkling water.

FOLLOW THE LEADER: If you're at a restaurant and you'd like to order an alcoholic beverage but you're uncertain as to whether or not you should do so, take your cue from those at your table. If the host orders a drink, then you may of course follow suit. If you are the first person asked, select something simple such as a soft drink. You can always change your order after hearing the selections of others by saying something like, "Oh, a glass of wine does sound nice; please change my soda order to wine." If you are hosting the meal, you may speak with your server in advance to instruct him as to which drinks you prefer to offer.

WHEN IN DOUBT, DON'T: When you're unsure if the other people at the gathering will be drinking, play it safe and order something nonalcoholic. Again, you are always free to change your order in the manner described above or for the second round.

THIS VS. THAT: While a mixed drink, a beer, and a glass of wine all have approximately the same alcohol content, you should consider your surroundings before choosing a beverage. Take note of what the other people in your party are drinking, and choose something similar. In general, a glass of wine is a safe bet. Please note that I did not mention shots. Shots are appropriate with dinner in only the most unusual of circumstances.

ENOUGH IS ENOUGH: During business interactions or instances in which you are meeting people for the first time, no matter how well you think you hold your liquor, I recommend limiting yourself to one drink. Nothing dispels a respectable image like slurring one's words, losing one's balance, or saying something inappropriate.

KNOW YOUR LIMITS

At a recent corporate function, I mentioned that few individuals improve upon their reputations (professional or social) with the increased consumption of alcohol. In response to my statement, a participant stood to announce that he had already had eight glasses of wine and was feeling fine. In addition to slurring his words, he lost his balance while trying to sit down (luckily he managed to catch himself on the edge of his chair). Needless to say, my point was made clear to the rest of the group.

GARNISH GUIDELINES: Such drink garnishes as lemon and lime wedges are meant to be pushed into the drink, not nibbled. The thin little straws that often appear in drinks are actually stirrers and should be removed as soon as possible.

TACKLING TRICKY FOODS

APPROACHING ARTICHOKES: Steamed artichokes served with a dipping sauce are properly eaten with your fingers. Gently but firmly pull out a leaf at a time and dip before eating the tender "meat" at the base of the leaf; the rough edge of the leaf (at the top end) should be discarded on your plate. When you arrive at the center, remove the fuzz with your knife. Then eat the heart of the artichoke using your fork and knife.

FRENCH ONION SOUP: This is a classic never-order on-a-first-date dish. While tasty, French onion soup is challenging to eat because of the dense, seemingly impenetrable layer of cheese on top. Usually, you are given only a soupspoon with which to work. To break through the cheese, press the side of the spoon against the inside of the bowl (with the cheese wedged between the two). While there are actually special cheese knives for eating French onion soup, few establishments keep these on hand. In the vast majority of situations, you are on your own with the spoon.

While you may be tempted to use your dinner knife, refrain from doing so.

LONG PASTAS: This group includes spaghetti, linguini, fettuccine, and angel hair pasta. It is considered barbaric to cut one's pasta. Instead, you should be provided with a large-bowled spoon to use as an anchor for your fork tines as you twirl one or two pasta strands at a time. This is a skill that may take some time to master, so practice at home before trying it in public.

THE WORLD IS YOUR OYSTER: Generally, oysters are served on the half shell and eaten with a small fork. In some more casual establishments and at the beach, oysters may be slurped directly (yet quietly) from their shells.

SLIPPERY SNAILS: When served in their shells, escargots (the French word for snails) may be accompanied by a special gripper designed to let you hold the shell firmly with one hand while using a small two pronged fork to extract the meat with the other.

HOW TO EAT A LOBSTER: This tricky process requires you to use your hands, a seafood fork, a dinner fork and knife, a nutcracker, and if you're smart, a bib.

REMOVING THE CLAWS: The first step in eating a lobster is to separate the claws from the rest of the body. To remove a claw, grasp the body with one hand so that the lobster remains steady on your plate and then twist the claw with your other hand.

CRACKING THE CLAWS: To crack a claw, hold it close to your plate with one hand while using a nutcracker in your other to break the shell. Extract the meat with your seafood fork, using a twisting motion. Place the empty shell on the side of your plate, or discard it in the bowl brought for this purpose. (While the claws must be removed before the tail, you may eat the claw meat before or after eating the tail.)

REMOVING THE TAIL: Grab the back of the lobster with one hand and flip it over so that the belly is exposed. With your other hand, grab the tail and twist it until it separates from the rest of the body. (The faint of heart discard the body, though some lobster lovers will extract meat from this section [see page 87].)

EXTRACTING THE TAIL MEAT: You may slice the tail meat out of the shell with your knife. Another method is to push the tail meat out in a swift motion through the cracked portion of the body shell. The tail meat is eaten with your dinner fork and knife. Keep an eye out for the small, black, veinlike component, which is actually the lobster's digestive tract and should be discarded.

from CLUELESS *to* CLASS ACT

THE BODY CAVITY: As previously mentioned, some people also eat the meat from the body cavity. To break the shell, use your nutcracker. This often takes a few tries, so don't let yourself get discouraged too quickly. In addition to some meat, you'll find a couple of elements that some consider to be delicacies—namely a greenish substance, which is the tomalley, and in female lobsters, a reddish substance, which is the roe. Not everyone chooses to partake of these.

THE LEGS: Some diners so enjoy the lobster meat that they do not want any to go to waste, so they turn to the legs. These may be removed with one swift yank or a twisting motion. Sometimes, the meat is fished out of the legs using a very thin seafood fork. In more casual settings, people crack the legs with their teeth to extract the meat; this latter method is fine for lobster bakes on the beach, but otherwise you should think twice. I would not recommend eating the legs in more formal situations. In fact, at some upscale restaurants, the legs will be removed in the kitchen.

//

CHAPTER FIVE

DATING DOS
and
DON'TS

\\

YOU HAVE A GOOD JOB, GREAT FRIENDS, maybe even a dog, but you feel as though something is missing. You're craving some companionship—not just hang-out companionship, but something with a romantic aspect. The lightbulb above your head flashes—it's time to date! As with all other interactions, there are certain guidelines you should follow in order to make dating a more pleasant experience.

FINDING *the* RIGHT ROMANTIC PARTNER

GET OFF THE COUCH: The chances of your dream date being delivered to your door are slim. You need to get out of the house and meet new people. Become involved in some activities that you enjoy, as this will allow you to interact with others who share your interests. You might take a wine tasting class, participate in a philanthropic project, or join a sports or social club. Another alternative is to sign up for classes that you think will have a high concentration of potential partners (perhaps cooking lessons or coed intermediate golf instruction).

CLICK ON LOVE: Online dating sites are a great way to source and screen potential dates. Be sure to use the sites as a means toward an end instead of the end unto itself. If you are spending hours reading and clicking, it is time to find a new hobby.

EVALUATE YOUR STANDARDS: Of course you should have a basic idea of the type of person you are looking for, and yes, you can use those sought-after qualities as a filter. But if you are finding that no one ever seems to pass your test, it might be time to rethink your standards. Or, perhaps, you are simply judging people too quickly.

KEEP AN OPEN MIND: While the thought of dating your grandmother's neighbor's second cousin once removed may not make your heart sing, a date is better than no date. Agree to meet a wide variety of people.

FORGO THE FAKE-OUT

Do not give a person false hope by giving a fake phone number. It is better to let someone down easy on the spot than to make her feel like a fool later. Find a gentle phrase that works for you: "I am flattered you would ask, but my life is terribly busy right now." Or, "You are so sweet, but I don't think we would make a good match."

LOOK TO THE HORIZON: When you were in high school, it was fine to date someone forever. As an adult, though, you should know what your timeline is for taking a relationship to the next level of commitment. If this is not the right person for you, it is time to end the relationship. Do not simply keep someone around until someone better comes along.

USE YOUR RESOURCES: Ask your married and committed friends if they know anyone you might like. People are often honored to act as amateur matchmakers. If your friends' friends turn out to be duds, take it to the next level. Subscribe to a dating website or a matchmaking service.

The FIRST DATE

TEN-MINUTE TELEPHONE TALK: Since the attraction factor is most powerful in person, don't spend a lot of time chatting on the phone before you have even met. A little bit of small talk should give way to scheduling a brief first date. After the time and place have been set, end the conversation. You can talk more once you get together.

FLEETING LOOKS: Often, the chronically single will become stymied by first impressions. So much so, they may resort to asking for a photograph prior to meeting anyone new. In addition to demonstrating shallowness, this method is simply not a good predictor of the quality of a future relationship. Looks can be highly deceiving (as can photographs, for that matter), and personalities have the ability to alter perceptions.

COFFEE, ICE CREAM, OR DRINKS: The best first dates with someone you don't already really know usually entail meeting for coffee, ice cream, or drinks. Like the introductory telephone conversation, this initial get-together should be relatively short—about thirty to forty-five minutes. This time frame allows you to talk a little bit about yourselves in person and to decide whether or not you'd like to go out again. If you feel like you're hitting it off, call the next day to schedule a second date.

DATES AND DIVERSIONS: For shier people, I recommend that the first date be a stroll through a historic neighborhood, a shopping district, a farmer's market, or some other area of interest. As you walk, the sights that you pass can provide a steady stream of topics for conversation, helping you to avoid those dreaded awkward silences.

REMOVE THE RÉSUMÉ: There is a tendency to turn the first date into an interview. Do not interrogate your date. And avoid spending too much time talking about your job. Stay away from the topic of past relationships until you have decided that you actually like this person. After a few dates, you can begin to reveal more about yourself. Until then, keep the conversation light.

TWO-WAY STREET: As in other types of social interactions, conversation should be a two-way street. While you don't want to grill your date, pose some questions to show interest. You might ask about favorite classic television shows, the one children's book still loved as an adult, a favorite artist, or the ideal vacation. In any case, don't monopolize the discussion by talking about yourself all night, as you'll come off as self-absorbed. (For more information about carrying on a conversation, see the section that begins on page 111.)

SECOND CHANCE: Most married people will tell you that their first impression of their current spouse was not 100 percent positive. Imagine if these people had not given their dates a second chance. Because first dates are pressure-filled, you're not necessarily getting a realistic impression of the other person. Unless your date did something horrific, give it a second chance. Hey, you never know.

KEEP YOUR PANTS ON: In these troubled times, going slow is advisable for so many reasons—moral, medical, and legal. Be sure you really know someone before becoming intimate. Take your time—you don't want to be seen as a cad.

DATING DYNAMICS

BEST FOOT FORWARD: This should be obvious, but you should be on your best behavior with a date (in fact, you should really be on your best behavior during all types of interactions). Dress appropriately, arrive on time, and have a positive disposition. Ten minutes after the date was supposed to begin is too late to call and cancel!

BEYOND YOUR CONTROL: On rare occasions, you may need to cancel a date because of some unavoidable situation or event. As soon as you find yourself in this position, call your date to say you won't be able to make it. When possible, reschedule while on the phone. If you're calling at the last minute due to an emergency, reschedule as soon as the immediate crisis has passed.

TABLE FOR TWO: Good table manners are essential to all good relationships (if you need a refresher, turn back to chapter 4). If you have proper manners, your date will pay attention to what you're saying. If you have poor table manners, your date will have a hard time noticing anything else!

GENTLEMANLY GESTURES: In general, your manners will convey a lot to your date. Open doors, pull out the chair, and assist with coats. These gentlemanly gestures require very little effort and can have a very high return.

SAFETY FIRST: When arranging logistics, you may offer to pick up your date at home, but for the first few dates, it is best to opt to meet out and about. Often, we do not want someone to know where we live until we are more comfortable. Watch for cues—eventually there will be a point where you will meet at each other's homes.

CLEANLINESS IS NEXT TO GODLINESS: If you will be picking up your date in your car, make sure that the interior is tidy. There should not be any food wrappers or other trash lying around. You should also make sure that the exterior is clean. If necessary, take your wheels to the car wash earlier that day. Similarly, if your date will be entering your home, clean up beforehand (just as you should before having any guest over).

HOW *to* ASK SOMEONE OUT

RESEARCH FIRST: The key to a successful date is advanced planning. Do a little research before deciding where to take your date. Read reviews, and ask for recommendations from friends. If you're taking someone out for a meal, you don't want to end up at a place where the service is lousy and the food unappetizing. As you weigh your options, take into account your budget and the atmosphere of the venue. Both of you should feel comfortable in the setting.

MULTIPLE CHOICE: When asking someone out for a meal, it is best to offer a choice of restaurants, since people have different tastes and eating habits. Most likely, your date will appreciate your consideration.

MONETARY MATTERS: The person who does the asking does the paying. So when you ask somone out on a date, you should pay for the outing (this includes taking care of any coat check and valet parking tips). If your date offers to pay for part, politely decline. After you've taken someone on a few dates, it's time to reciprocate; she should ask you out or invite you over for a home-cooked meal.

SEVENTY-TWO-HOUR RULE: In the romantic realm, you must ask someone out at least three days in advance. So, if you'd like the pleasure of someone's company on Saturday night, you should call by Wednesday. (Yes, call. Texting for a date is just tacky.) Asking later makes you seem at best disorganized, at worst desperate to find a substitute for someone who canceled on you at the last minute.

NO ROOM FOR INTERPRETATION: Do not leave the other person wondering if you are splitting the bill or not. When asking someone out on a date, do so in the clearest possible way. "Alexia, I would like to take you to lunch on Tuesday." Or, "Sophia, it would be an honor if you would be my guest for lunch Saturday afternoon."

CALL FOR CONFIRMATION: The day before or morning of the get-together, call your date to confirm the logistics. And, if you're going out for a meal, call the restaurant to confirm the reservations.

TERRIFIC TIMING: Arrive a bit early at your meeting point so that your date is not put in the position of waiting for you. If you're picking your date up at home, arrive early (to make sure you're not late), but don't ring the bell until the appointed hour.

CULINARY CLUES: When dining out, don't leave your date guessing how many courses to order. Give some subtle hints. For instance, you might say, "Jennifer, the asparagus ravioli appetizer is out of this world" to indicate that you plan to order something to start.

BE ENTERTAINING: When you've invited someone on a date, it is up to you to direct the conversation. Have a few topics prepared in advance. Current events, the latest best-selling novel, or the latest movie you saw are all appropriate subjects to get the ball rolling.

ENDING *a* RELATIONSHIP

FACE THE MUSIC: It turns out there was no love connection, but you are dreading the conversation. Uncomfortable as it may be, you must bite the bullet and have the conversation. Avoiding calls, breaking up via text or changing your status on social media are not gentlemanly behaviors.

THE METHOD: Unless you've only been on a few dates, you must break up in person (the exception being if you are in a long-distance relationship and this is not feasible). While a public place is ideal, choose carefully. A five-star restaurant is not the setting for such a conversation, but a coffee shop or a local park will suit your needs.

SPARE THE GORY DETAILS: The way she sipped her wine may have made you sick, but this is a detail you should keep to yourself. Share a bit of the positive ("you are so much fun to be with"), but identify the disconnect ("my cat allergy does not bode well for the future given your love of Whiskers"). Wish her well, and end the interaction. It's best to keep this type of conversation brief, though the longer you've been dating, the more of an explanation you'll need to provide.

YOU'RE NOT THE ONE: It may be that someone you've been seeing wants to break up with you. If you are able to take this news calmly, wonderful. If it fills you with venom, do not act in a mean-spirited way. While it may be tempting to post nasty-a-grams, resist this impulse. You'll be better off, and happier, in the long run.

CHAPTER SIX

PERSONAL APPEARANCE

MARKETING EXECUTIVES KNOW THAT it's all about packaging when it comes to selling a product. Similarly, when you get dressed, you are selling yourself to the world. What is it that you are saying about yourself? Is it the message you want to send? Like it or not, the way you appear to others sets a tone for your interactions and the way in which others treat you. The key is to think about the people you are going to come into contact with and use your image to your advantage by making the best impression possible.

IMPROVING YOUR IMAGE

CREATING YOUR COSTUME: Think of your closet as a wardrobe department. Before you choose an outfit, consider what role you are going to play that day—corporate executive (tailored suit, assuming the office isn't business casual), academic (tweed blazer), international playboy (tuxedo). Take the time to consider what messages you are sending to others.

TAKE IT UP A NOTCH: While it would be nice if we always knew exactly what to wear, it is not always so easy to decipher the dress code. If you are in a position to comfortably do so, ask someone about the appropriate attire. If not, the rule of thumb is that it is better to be overdressed than underdressed.

OPEN STANCE: A person's body language mirrors his confidence level. Those who are nervous or unsure tend to slouch, fidget, and avoid eye contact. To project a favorable image, stand with your shoulders back, arms at your side, and head up. Be sure to make eye contact—failure to do so may lead others to think you have something to hide.

YOU'RE NEVER FULLY DRESSED WITHOUT A . . . : Smile. People would much rather speak with someone who is smiling than someone who is scowling.

CHOOSE YOUR WORDS: Making a good impression also entails being aware of what you say. Think before you speak, and speak in positive terms about those around you. Avoid foul language and slang.

ELECTRONIC SECURITY: When out and about, your cell phone is not an electronic security blanket. It must be out of your hands and out of sight. Your focus should be on the people who are with you. Perpetually checking your mobile device makes you seem immature and insecure. Put it away until you are alone again.

GOOD GROOMING

FRESH FACE: Whenever you plan to have contact with the outside world, you'll need to perform some critical grooming. If you don't have a beard and/or moustache, you must shave. If you do have a beard and/or moustache, you should trim your facial hair. For those of you who start to sport a five o'clock shadow at 11:00 a.m., consider obtaining and carrying a travel shaving kit so that you're looking your best for those important meetings or dates that will be taking place later in the day.

NEW ARRIVALS: As you grow older, hair will start to appear in places you never thought possible. Trim your nose and ear hairs. Look critically at your eyebrows and knuckles. If the word "werewolf" comes to mind, it's time to trim.

MINTY FRESH: There are few situations as unpleasant as being face-to-face with someone who has bad breath. Make sure that you are never the cause of such unpleasantness. Have a breath spray, mints, or dissolvable strips on hand at all times.

A HINT OF MINT

Should you find yourself in the company of someone with bad breath and you can't grin and bear it, take a mint for yourself in front of that person and offer him one (after all, you're only being polite by sharing). And if someone at some point offers you a mint, take it.

HANDSOME HANDS: Eyes may be the windows to the soul, but hands are the gatekeepers. Nails should be cut to the quick, and hands (including the area underneath the nails) should be clean. Men get manicures, too.

MAN OF MYSTERY: All aspects of grooming should be taken care of in private. These activities are not for public viewing.

NAIL NOTICE: Just in case you weren't sure, clipping fingernails and toenails is an aspect of personal grooming and thus should never be done in public. Not only is the action itself offensive to others, but no one wants to be confronted with the nail clippings that you leave behind.

DON'T YA BLOW: If your nose is running, a dab from a handkerchief is acceptable when in public. If you have a terrible cold and need to blow your nose, you should excuse yourself and find a restroom. (If you need to blow your nose more than six times an hour, you are probably sick enough to warrant staying home.)

PICK IN PRIVATE: You should never engage in behavior that will disgust others. If you need to clean your ears or scratch inside your nose, find a restroom or wait until you are home.

OLFACTORY FATIGUE: You may love your aftershave. Your significant other may love your aftershave. But the rest of the population shouldn't know whether they love your aftershave; if someone who isn't close enough to hug you can smell it, you're wearing too much.

FOLLICLE FIX: As you grow older, your hair will change—in terms of both texture and amount. If you are attempting to pull off the haircut you had while in high school, chances are it's high time for a change. Have someone new cut your hair.

LESS REQUIRES MORE: If you notice that you're beginning to lose your hair, take the time to find an expert stylist. This stylist will be able to work with you and your hair to make the most of what you've got. As I am sure you have already realized, the comb-over does not fool anyone. Not even you.

FACE YOUR NEEDS

If you have yet to do so, treat yourself to a facial. (If you think that facials are just for women, think again.) Find out what type of skin you have and what products are best for taking care of it. If unwanted hair is an issue, you should know that many facialists also do waxing.

from CLUELESS *to* CLASS ACT

APPROPRIATE ATTIRE

CLOSET MUST-HAVES: You should own a dark suit, a white button-down shirt, a coordinating dress tie, matching dress shoes (such as wingtips or oxfords), and a coordinating belt. Such an ensemble is handy not only for job interviews but for presentations, most religious services (including funerals), and some weddings.

COMFORT CLOTHING: Anytime that you're out in public—even if you're running errands—you should look presentable. Obviously, this doesn't mean you have to pull out a suit and tie, but you shouldn't be looking grungy either. You never know whom you might run into . . .

GYM WEAR: If you work out regularly at the gym, you should purchase clothing specifically designed for this activity. Ratty sweatpants and fraying T-shirts should be saved for gardening. And please remember to launder them after each and every wearing.

NEVER WEAR: You should never leave the house in anything that has a stain, hole, or tear; is missing buttons; is too tight; or went out of style a decade ago.

TIME FRAME

If you wear eyeglasses, I recommend updating your frames every one to two years—you don't want to be walking around with glasses that are obviously out of style. Since you and those around you undoubtedly know the importance of maintaining eye contact, others will be spending a good deal of time looking at your eyes and, hence, your glasses. I know that new frames aren't cheap, but considering the amount of time you spend wearing them and the impact that they have on your appearance, they're a wise investment.

WHAT LIES BENEATH: Do not overlook the importance of an undershirt, which will prevent your perspiration from staining your outer shirt. A white undershirt is a requirement anytime you wear a white dress shirt.

SHINE THOSE SHOES: There are still those among us who judge a man by his shoes. Be sure to keep yours in tip-top shape. They should be clean, polished, and in good condition (not worn out). Because shoes are hardworking articles, they need to be well cared for and replaced regularly.

from CLUELESS *to* CLASS ACT

GETTING FORMAL

TUX TALK: If you're invited to a black-tie affair, you'll need a tuxedo. Fortunately, you have the option of renting if you don't own one. A tuxedo jacket may be single-breasted or double-breasted (the former has a single line of buttons down the front, while the latter has two parallel lines of buttons).

SINGLE VS. DOUBLE: The double-breasted tuxedo jacket looks best when you're standing and, hence, is a good choice for cocktail parties. If the event will involve sitting, the single-breasted jacket is more practical, since its design will better accommodate you should you wish to undo the bottom buttons for greater comfort while sitting. (When a double-breasted jacket is unbuttoned, there is a lot of material flapping around.) Double-breasted jackets generally have four buttons, though they may have fewer or more. The number of buttons on a single-breasted suit tends to vary with fashion trends, though two or three buttons is considered classic.

LOVE THOSE LAPELS: You'll also have a choice of lapel style—peaked, notched, or shawl (see illustrations on page 107)—when selecting a tuxedo jacket. Which one you choose is really a matter of fashion as opposed to appropriateness.

THE TAILCOAT: The front of this coat stops short at the waist, while the back extends to the knees. The tails take the shape of a long, thin U with a single vent. The tailcoat is properly worn with a waistcoat, which is a specific type of vest that tends to be cut lower in the front than others. This style of tuxedo is usually worn in the most formal of settings.

CUT TO THE CUTAWAY: This coat gently yet quickly slopes away from the waist in the front to a broad tail in the back, which—as in the tailcoat—extends to the wearer's knees. The cutaway is worn with a specific type of vest designed to accompany it. Morning coats are often cutaways in the slightly less formal color of gray and are intended for daytime wear.

SINGLE-BREASTED

DOUBLE-BREASTED

TAILCOAT

CUTAWAY

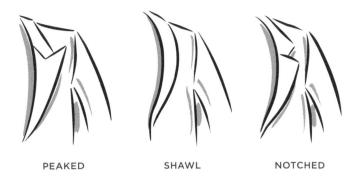

PEAKED   SHAWL   NOTCHED

THE SHIRT ON YOUR BACK: Shirts designed for formal-wear may be plain or pleated in the front (some are even ruffled, though whether or not you should wear such a design depends on current fashion trends). The two most common collar options are the turndown collar and the wing collar. The turndown is similar to the collars on shirts that one would wear to the office. When you wear a shirt with this type of collar, the bow tie rests on the outside of the collar. A wing collar has two small "wings" projecting downward. As you tie your bow tie, the wings are raised so that they point toward your face; once the bow tie is in place, the wings are folded down and tucked behind the bow. The wing collar is more formal than the turndown.

CUFF HIM: You'll also have options when it comes to shirt cuffs, which may or may not have buttons. French cuffs—considered a more formal option—have holes for cuff links instead of buttons.

BOW TIE BASICS: When wearing a tuxedo for an evening affair, the bow tie is a necessary accessory. A white bow tie is worn for ultraformal occasions (along with a tailcoat, a white waistcoat or vest, and a wing-collared shirt). A black tie is the second most formal possibility. Your bow tie should match your vest or cummerbund.

HOW TO TIE A BOW TIE: The ability to tie a bow tie is a challenging skill that separates the men from the gentlemen. If you have not done this before, don't despair if your first attempt is laughable. Keep trying until you feel comfortable with the motions. Practice makes perfect.

> **STEP ONE:** Place the bow tie around your neck leaving one side (X) between one to two inches longer than the other side (Y).

> **STEP TWO:** Take side "X" and cross it over side "Y."

> **STEP THREE:** Pull "X" up behind "Y."

> **STEP FOUR:** With "X" still pointing up toward your chin, fold "Y" in half to form the first part of the bow.

> **STEP FIVE:** Fold "X" down over "Y."

> **STEP SIX:** Hold the first part of the bow in place with one hand, and use the other to push "X" up and behind the first part of the bow to form the second side of the bow.

> **STEP SEVEN:** Gently adjust the bow tie so that both sides are even.

STEP ONE

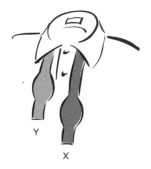

Y

X

STEP TWO

STEP THREE

STEP FOUR

STEP FIVE

STEP SIX

STEP SEVEN

COOL AS A CUMMERBUND: If you're not wearing a waist-coat or vest, you most likely will wear a cummerbund. Make sure the pleats are facing up.

PANTS WITH PANACHE: Tuxedo pants have either one or two stripes down the outside seam of each leg. These stripes are the same color as the pants, but made from a different fabric. Tuxedo pants do not have cuffs.

FANCY FOOTWORK: The shoes worn with tuxedos are usually patent leather slip-ons. Other footwear options include a basic oxford made of patent leather.

CHAPTER SEVEN

MEETING *and* GREETING

AH, THE ART OF SMALL TALK. SOMETIMES it seems as though certain people were born with the gift of gab. But the truth of the matter is that being a good conversationalist is actually a learned skill. This means that with a bit of coaching and practice anyone can mingle like a pro. So what are the basics for meeting and greeting? Read on.

CARRYING
on a
CONVERSATION

KNOW YOURSELF: Always be prepared to give a self introduction. Your name gets you only halfway there. You should also include a little something about yourself—it is this shared fact that will propel the conversation, cuing the other person to ask you a question. "Hi, I am Lee Santos, brother of the bride." "Nice to meet you. I am Ian Bannerman from Boston." "Hello, I am Harry Schuler. I'm today's speaker."

INTRODUCING OTHERS: The basic rule is that men are introduced to women, younger people are introduced to older people, and lower-ranking individuals are introduced to higher-ranking individuals. When making an introduction, include each person's full name and mention something that the parties may have in common to help the conversation start. For instance, "Miss Burr, may I introduce Mr. Jacob Alhart. Jacob, this is Marion Burr; she just returned from Belize." Or, "Grandmother, this is my roommate Nolan Samberg. Nolan, this is my grandmother, Ms. Eleanor Calvin. Grandmother, Nolan has just finished writing a novel."

FOR OPENERS: When you are introduced to someone new, meet her gaze, shake her hand (see page 117 for instructions on how to do this properly), and say that you're pleased to meet her.

from CLUELESS *to* CLASS ACT

BE PREPARED: Before going to any event, have a few backup topics of conversation on hand so that you have something to say should a lull in the conversation occur. There are many appropriate topics, such as current events, movies, plays, concerts, books, school/work, hobbies, family, travel, sports, and pets. Choose the ones that most interest you. When in doubt, you can always talk about the weather!

PARTY TRICK

Before attending a cocktail party or a similar type of gathering that involves mingling, have a snack. You don't want to be distracted during conversations by hunger. It's challenging to be witty when you're starving. And shoveling food into your mouth is certainly no way to meet new people.

PLAY CATCH: Think of conversation as a game of catch. You catch the ball, hold on to it for a few seconds, then throw it back to the other person, who catches it, holds on to it for a few seconds, then throws it back to you. This process is then repeated. Good conversations involve give and take. If you find that you are not talking at all or that you are doing all of the talking, something is off.

KEEP THE GAME GOING: Just as it affects the image you project, body language can go a long way toward keeping a conversation going. Your body should face the other person, shoulders squared to hers; your stance should be open, rather than closed off (in other words, don't cross your arms or hide your hands in your pockets). Last but not least, maintain gentle eye contact. All of these actions indicate to the other person that you are receptive and interested in what she has to say.

ALL EARS: Make sure that the other person knows that you're listening. The message can be conveyed by nodding your head or by voicing an occasional "um-hum."

CONTINUOUS CONVERSATION: Another way to keep the conversation flowing involves the way you phrase things. Be sure to ask open-ended questions—ones that require at least a sentence as an answer. "How do you know the host?" "What makes you say that?" "What was your favorite vacation?" "Tell me about . . ."

THE RECEIVING END: When asked a question, avoid giving a monosyllabic answer. Even if the person asks a "yes or no" question, expand upon your response with some sort of explanation to keep the conversation rolling. Do not put the other person in the position of having to do all the work by giving only one-word answers. If the conversation seems boring to you, change the subject to one that interests you more.

FLASH THOSE PEARLY WHITES: As mentioned with regard to general appearance, smiling is important. Good conversationalists know how to smile. Wouldn't you rather speak to someone who is smiling than someone who isn't?

TIMING IS EVERYTHING: Most cocktail party conversations (and other discussions that take place in social situations where everyone is standing up and mingling) should last, on average, about five to eight minutes. Remember, this is a chance for you to meet new people, not close a business deal or set a wedding date.

COCKTAIL COORDINATION

Cocktail party situations are ideal for people who are left-handed. I like to say that at cocktail-style events, everyone is a lefty. You should carry your food or your drink in your left hand so that your right is free to shake hands and exchange business cards.

INFORMATION EXCHANGE: If you have enjoyed speaking with someone, go ahead and exchange contact information before ending the conversation. Ask for the individual's business card so that you can get in touch at a later date. Once the person has handed you his card, offer yours. Note, however, that you should never offer your card first. Carry your business cards with you wherever you go—you never know when someone will ask you for one.

GRACEFUL EXITS: While often considered one of the most awkward aspects of social interactions, once learned, extricating yourself from a conversation is a remarkably simple task. As the conversation begins to lag, look the person in the eye, extend your right hand for a handshake, and say, "It was a pleasure to meet you." You could also use "I enjoyed speaking with you" or "It was great to catch up." Any pleasantry that indicates the conversation is over will do.

EXCUSES TO ESCHEW: When trying to remove yourself from a conversation, don't tell the other person that you're going to the bar, as he may decide to join you. Also, never say that you need to use the facilities. First of all, this is more information than a new acquaintance needs to know. Second, do you really want your encounter to end on a note that involves your bladder?

MAINTAIN CONTROL: Being the one to bring a conversation to a close gives you control as to how it ends. This is especially important if you don't want to share contact information. Extricate yourself before the discussion gets to that point.

BUDDY SYSTEM: If you're attending an event with a friend, work the room alone. After all, if the two of you wanted to talk to each other, you could have done that at home. Mingling on your own will not only force you to speak to others, but also encourage others to speak to you—it is often too intimidating for individuals to break into a conversation that is already in progress. Do check in with your buddy periodically, though. You may even want to establish some signals to indicate when you're ready to leave.

SHYNESS AND SOCIAL SITUATIONS

A large part of life involves speaking with other people. If you are truly very shy, you should enroll in an adult education course or volunteer at your favorite charity, since the more you put yourself in situations where you will be interacting with others, the more practice you will have speaking with others and the better you will feel. Sometimes part of confidence is simply faking it until you feel it. You could also join one of the many organizations that offer training in public speaking and interacting with others.

HANDSHAKES

FIRST CONTACT: One of the most basic social skills is the ability to shake hands well. While few people will admit to giving a bad handshake, almost everyone has been on the receiving end of one at some point in their lives.

TOUCHY SUBJECT: "Cold and clammy" is not the impression you want to make when meeting someone or encountering an acquaintance. If you have just come in from the cold, take a moment to warm up before coming into contact with others.

WEB TO WEB: The "web" between your index finger and thumb should hit the web of the other person.

FINGER CURL: Your fingers should then curl around the bottom of the other person's hand.

PROPER PRESSURE: You should apply enough pressure to the other person's hand that this individual can feel you are there, but not so much as to make his knees buckle. Shaking hands is not the time to show off your brute strength.

SHAKE, SHAKE: Shake the other person's hand up and down two or three times before releasing. The motion should be controlled, but natural. If the other person is thrown off balance or looks as though he's trying to pump water, you are being too vigorous and should tone it down a bit.

BEGINNING AND END: For those occasions during which it is appropriate to shake hands, you should shake at the beginning of the interaction and then again at the end.

THEN AND NOW

Back in the olden days, a man would not extend his hand to a woman unless she extended hers first. Nowadays, we are gender neutral, but the etiquette of shaking hands is all about rank and age. The highest-ranking or older person should extend his hand first. (Note that this does not always happen, and occasionally the lower-ranking person will be penalized for not shaking the boss's hand.)

TABOO TOPICS

BACKGROUND BASICS: It is best not to comment on someone's race or ethnic background (or even ask where the person is from) unless the individual has raised the topic. Even asking about someone's accent can be perceived as an inapproporiate question.

INDIVIDUAL IDENTITY: A person's religion or cultural heritage can prove to be a highly charged topic. Again, unless the individual has brought up the subject, avoid this area. There are those who try to push their own point of view, hoping to influence a person in her choice of religion or cultural identification. In the vast majority of situations, it is simply unacceptable to proselytize to a new acquaintance.

BANDAGES AND BRACES: As tempted as you may be, do not ask what any bandages or devices that provide physical assistance are for, as this is none of your business. If the individual cares to discuss his medical history with you, he'll bring it up.

AND BABY MAKES THREE: Unless you are a very close friend, do not ask a couple when they plan to have children.

BIG-TICKET ITEMS: When someone tells you she has purchased a house, a car, or tickets for a cruise around the world, if your natural reaction is to play "The Price Is Right," bite your tongue. It is not polite to ask. Your curiosity can come across as tacky or jealous behavior.

//

CHAPTER EIGHT

EVERYDAY *and* EVERY-SO-OFTEN ENCOUNTERS

\\

WHEN WE ARE IN SITUATIONS THAT WE aren't familiar with, we sometimes run the risk of offending an individual without intending any harm. We may have the best of intentions, but our lack of experience causes us to do or say the wrong thing. Some of us, for instance, may not have had much contact with people who are ill, pregnant, or physically challenged. But by becoming educated in the proper manners, we can demonstrate respect in such interactions.

ETIQUETTE *of* ILLNESS

FEAR FACTOR: Many wonderful, strong, courageous men go weak in the knees at the thought of visiting a person who is ill. While it is rarely fun to visit someone who is sick, it's certainly no fun being sick and lonely. As an adult, it is your duty to visit a friend or relative who is ill. Put the other individual's needs ahead of your own feelings.

MAKE AN OFFER: Instead of saying "Call if you need anything," offer to perform some specific service. The former approach places a burden on someone to figure out what it is that you can do to help; it also puts this person in the often uncomfortable position of having to ask. Those in need will be much more likely to take you up on an offer if it is for a specific action.

CALL AHEAD: Before stopping by, call to make sure that the person is up for a visit. If your presence is welcome, offer to bring something specific. Some appropriate options are food (perhaps Chinese takeout or pizza, if the person's condition permits) or some form of entertainment (a book, a magazine, a movie, a crossword puzzle, a board game, a deck of cards, or hobby supplies, for example).

GERMS BE GONE: As soon as you arrive at a sick person's home or the hospital, wash your hands to diminish the risk of spreading germs. If you're not 100 percent healthy, call the person (or the caregiver) to find out if you should still come.

SHORT AND SWEET: Unless otherwise indicated by the patient, keep the visit short so as not to tire him out. Whenever possible, end each visit by scheduling the next time you plan to stop by. Doing so will give the individual something to look forward to in the days to come.

ALWAYS ASK: You should always ask, "How are you?" in a sympathetic tone. Then take your cues from the patient's response as to whether further discussion about the condition is wanted. Some patients find it easier to share their feelings with people outside their immediate circle, as they don't want to upset those close to them. Above all, you should be a good listener.

CAREFUL CONVERSATIONS: If the patient has been laid up for a while, there may not be much she can add to the conversation. Come with amusing anecdotes to share. Stay away from "sicker than thou" stories, as these rarely make anyone feel better. Try to keep the discussion light and upbeat.

MAKE YOURSELF USEFUL: When someone is sick, the daily chores tend to pile up. If you have the time, you might help out with the "three Cs": cooking, cleaning, and caring. For instance, you could bring in or cook meals, do some grocery shopping, walk the dog, clean the house, carpool the kids, take care of the laundry, or mow the lawn.

When someone is ill, there is often an army of people assisting in the care. Whenever possible, recognize those helpers by thanking them for their efforts. Caring for others is a difficult, draining, and often underappreciated task. A few kind words can mean a lot. A gift basket can mean even more. If the person is a professional caregiver or a hospital staff member, a letter to his supervisor is true praise indeed.

CALLED TO SERVE: In your community, if the word goes out that someone needs help, you should not hesitate to volunteer. While you may not know the person, he may welcome new visitors. An alternative to visiting is to take care of some necessary task or errand that will help take some pressure off the person in need.

CONSTANT COMMUNICATION: Even if someone who is ill does not respond, or is unable to respond, you should still keep in touch. You can send cards, notes, e-mails, letters, flowers, fruit baskets, articles of interest, or pictures. Such small gestures can be the highlight of someone's day.

DON'T DO NOTHING: Some of us are just so uncomfortable around someone who is sick that we try to avoid the situation altogether. Other times we are afraid of overstepping our bounds or invading the person's privacy. But it is important to do something. Just the fact that you made an effort lets someone know that you care.

ETIQUETTE *and* EXPECTANT COUPLES

DON'T ASK: Even if you're 99.9 percent positive that she is, never ask a woman if she's pregnant. If she isn't, she'll likely be insulted. And even if she is, she might not be ready to tell you or others.

THINK BEFORE YOU SPEAK: Once you know a woman is pregnant, do not share any horrific tales of pregnancy or birth that you've heard. Trust me, she's already worried enough about having a healthy baby. Reassurances of what a good mother she will make, however, will most likely be appreciated.

DON'T TOUCH: As tempting as it may be, that round belly is still part of the woman's body. Unless she has invited you to do so, don't touch.

SUDDENLY SUPERSTITIOUS: Many people are superstitious during pregnancy, so don't be offended if you find the parents-to-be reluctant to discuss the baby. Some couples who are expecting won't tell others the baby's name or gender. Many also prefer not to have a baby shower until after the birth.

BOYS AT THE BABY SHOWER

As fathers take more and more of an active role in the lives of their children (and with same-sex couples having families), men have started to be included in the baby shower. And when the father attends, other men are invited too. Typically, this celebration is a midday event with light refreshments, though sometimes brunch or lunch is offered. The main activity is watching the expectant parents open gifts for the baby. Presents generally include baby clothing, toys, books, diapers, and other baby supplies. If you attend, you'll be expected to arrive with a gift. Luckily for you, many couples register (feel free to ask the host of the shower or the parents-to-be). If the couple is indeed registered, select something within your price range. Beware: many coed baby showers also involve games. This may include timed diapering of dolls, identifying the flavors of different baby foods while blindfolded, and/ or playing trivia games that revolve around—you guessed it—babies. Be a good sport and play along.

ACKNOWLEDGE LOSS: If a woman has a miscarriage or the baby is stillborn, as awkward and difficult as the situation may be, you should share your sympathies with the couple. It is during the most difficult of times that people need to know you care. Understand that each person reacts to this type of loss differently. Reach out, but then respond based upon the individual's cues.

BABY'S ARRIVAL

AND THEN THERE WERE THREE: Once the baby is born, don't go to the hospital without calling first to make sure that the new family is accepting visitors. Bring a small gift; flowers or food for the new parents or a stuffed animal for the baby are easy options (keep in mind that latex balloons are not allowed in most hospitals for safety reasons). When you arrive, wash your hands before getting anywhere near the baby. And keep the visit short (no longer than fifteen to twenty minutes) so as not to tire out the new parents, who are undoubtedly already exhausted.

PICTURE OF PERFECT HEALTH: If this heading does not describe you, don't visit a newborn or the family. You don't want to risk spreading infection. Even if you have only a sniffle, stay away.

SEND SOMETHING: If you're unable to visit, a bouquet of flowers is a welcome addition to the decor of any hospital room. Many hospitals have in-house florist shops from which you can order if you're not familiar with local providers.

NEW PARENTS

BIRTH ANNOUNCEMENTS: If you receive a birth announcement, you are not required to send a present, but it is a gentlemanly gesture to send a card.

BABY TALK: Since new parents are usually in awe of their child (with good reason), you might as well make the baby the topic of conversation. If you're at a loss for what to say, you may ask about the little one's disposition, sleeping habits, and how the couple chose the baby's name.

PREOCCUPIED PARENTS: Understand that new parents tend to have a difficult time holding up their end of the conversation. Between the overwhelming new responsibilities of taking care of a completely dependent little being and the lack of sleep, focusing on others can be quite challenging. Be sympathetic if the conversation does not flow.

SO CUTE: Yes, babies are irresistible to many. But beware about touching an infant. First-time parents are especially cautious. Always ask first. And if the parents would prefer you refrain, respect their wishes. Don't feel offended.

BEYOND PINK AND BLUE: Yes, even if you have given a present at a baby shower, a small gift is appropriate if you visit the family after the baby is home. When choosing a gift for a baby, feel free to pick colors beyond the typical pink and blue. Green, yellow, and purple are all wonderful for babies. You might also consider giving your favorite childhood book.

ASSISTING PEOPLE
with PHYSICAL
CHALLENGES

OFFER FIRST: When interacting with someone who you think might need your help, offer your assistance and wait for the individual to accept. Don't touch anyone before your offer has been accepted.

BLINDNESS: To offer assistance to a blind person, you should verbally address him as you approach and ask to help. Most blind people who accept will expect you to move to their right and offer your left elbow so that they can follow your lead. Do not grab a person's arm and push him along.

DEAFNESS: When speaking to someone who has hearing loss, look directly at her. If the individual has a hearing aid or reads lips, this position will make it easier for her to understand you.

WHEELCHAIR USE: Often the best assistance you can provide for a person in a wheelchair is clearing a path that will permit navigation. When speaking to someone in a wheelchair, try to find a seat for yourself so that the individual is not forced to endure a conversation looking up at you.

MIND YOUR MANNERS: When meeting a person who is physically challenged, no matter how curious you are, do not ask about the disability. If he wants to share this information with you, he will do so on his own. And for goodness' sake, don't stare.

CHAPTER NINE

HERE
to
THERE

THE TRUEST TEST OF A MAN'S CHARACTER is the way he behaves when in motion. As you enter a building, do you open the door for others? When you're on a train, do you offer your seat to someone less able-bodied than yourself? On the elevator, do you move over to make room for those wishing to enter? It is the way we treat those we don't know that is often most telling about our true nature. What do your actions say about you?

TRADITIONAL DOORS

OPEN SESAME: When approaching a closed door—whether it leads to a residence or a private office—you must knock (or ring the doorbell) and then wait to be invited inside. Do not barge inside.

ALLOW ME: When you are approaching a door with another individual, the younger, lower-ranking, or more able-bodied person should open the door for the older, higher-ranking, or less able-bodied person.

LADIES FIRST

Back in the days when chivalry reigned, a man would always open the door for a woman. Then there was great social upheaval, and chivalrous men became the recipients of evil looks and snide remarks when they performed this gesture. Fortunately, our society has progressed beyond this stage, and most women know this action does not imply that a woman is too frail to open the door herself, but rather is a sign of respect. So go forth and open!

HOLD ON: Be sure to hold the door for anyone who may be behind you (and take a quick glance over your shoulder to avoid accidentally letting the door close in someone's face).

RIGHT OF WAY: When people heading in opposite directions arrive at a doorway, those who are already inside the building or room must be allowed to exit before those who are on their way in may enter.

REVOLVING DOORS

WHO'S FIRST? When a revolving door is already in motion, the older, higher-ranking, or less able-bodied person should enter first. When this type of door is not already moving, the younger, lower-ranking, or more able-bodied person should enter first to set the door in motion.

KEEP MOVING: When you are exiting on the other side, do not stop directly in front of the revolving door, as the people behind you will have nowhere to go. If you are unsure as to which direction your destination is, step aside to figure it out so that you don't cause a pileup.

PULL YOUR WEIGHT: Unless you are physically unable to do so, once you've entered a revolving door, you are responsible for doing your share of the pushing—there are no free rides. That said, this is not an amusement park; be aware of those around you, and do not send the door whipping around.

ELEVATOR ETIQUETTE

RIGHT OF WAY: Let those who are trying to exit an elevator do so before you attempt to step into it. Following this simple practice will make the process easier for everyone involved.

TAKE CONTROL: If you're the person closest to the control panel, offer to press buttons for other passengers.

HOLD IT: If you see another person coming, hold the elevator. How would you feel if the situation were reversed and no one held the elevator for you? Do unto others . . .

NO HOLDUPS: If you run to catch the elevator and find other passengers inside, yet the rest of your group is trailing behind you, let the elevator go and wait for the next one. Undoubtedly, those already inside are in as much of a hurry as you.

PATIENCE IS A VIRTUE: The elevator does not go any faster just because you keep pressing the button. The only effect this action may have is to irritate those around you.

TO SPEAK OR NOT TO SPEAK: If you're carrying on a conversation with someone in an elevator, beware of what you say. Don't say anything that can't be repeated—even if you don't know the other passengers. Also do not subject your fellow riders—who can't escape until they reach their floors—to any discussion that they might find unpleasant (no one wants to hear about your gastrointestinal issues or half of your cell phone conversation). Last but not least, keep your voice down; in such tight quarters there's no reason to shout.

HAVE A NICE DAY: Engaging in small talk with other passengers can be pleasant, but it is not required.

EASY EXITS: If you're at the front of a crowded elevator, when the doors open at a floor, step out to allow others to exit. If you are in the back and must get by others to exit, say "Excuse me." Do not push or shove.

ESCALATORS

PICK A LANE: Although there's no painted line, there are definitely lanes on escalators. Those simply standing should stay on the right, while those who wish to pass should do so on the left.

DON'T HESITATE: Proceed swiftly when stepping onto or off of an escalator. If you suddenly slow down or stop, the people behind you have no option but to bump into you. When stepping off, if you are confused as to which direction you need to head, move aside before stopping to figure it out.

GET A TREADMILL: As tempting as it may be to run up the down escalator or run down the up escalator, refrain from doing so. Not only do you run the risk of injuring others, but those teeth at the edge of the escalator steps can be dangerous.

PEDESTRIAN PROTOCOL

OUT OF HARM'S WAY: When you are walking down the sidewalk with a date, you should position yourself between your companion and moving traffic. When you are walking with children, you should position yourself between the children and the moving traffic. Safety first.

WALK WITH A PURPOSE: Walk with your head up, shoulders back, and eyes taking in your surroundings. Let your arms swing gently, or allow them to rest at your side.

TRAVELING IN A PACK: When you're walking down the street in a group, make sure that others can move around you. Don't monopolize the sidewalk.

DON'T BLOCK TRAFFIC: If for any reason you decide to stop on the sidewalk (perhaps to talk to a friend or figure out where you're going), step out of the way so that you don't hinder others.

WALK AND TALK: For some inexplicable reason, some pedestrians can't seem to talk or text while walking in a straight line; instead they wander from side to side as though they've had a little too much to drink. If you're going to talk on your cell phone while walking on the sidewalk, don't let it interfere with your forward progress. Be aware of those around you. (Also, note that if you make a call from the street, there is bound to be a lot of background noise, which the person on the other end might find disturbing.)

AIRPLANES

HIGH STYLE: I love the pictures of passengers during the early days of air travel. The people always look as though they're going to a party. Nowadays, travelers look (and sometimes smell) as though they've come directly from the gym. Considering the cramped quarters of most planes, do your best to ensure that your attire will not offend your fellow passengers. (Keep in mind, too, that even if you're traveling to or from a warm climate, the temperature on airplanes tends to be cool, so dressing in layers is your best bet for comfort.)

SIZE MATTERS: While it would be nice if there were unlimited space for luggage in the passenger cabin, this is simply not the case. Bring on board only what you are positive will fit in the overhead storage compartment or underneath the seat.

FOOD FOR THOUGHT: If you're bringing your own sustenance onto the plane, avoid foods with odors that other passengers might find offensive, such as tuna.

KNOW YOUR BOUNDARIES: When seated, do not let your limbs, personal belongings, or blanket spill over to another person's seat. Most likely, the person sitting next to you spent a good deal of money—or forked over a lot of frequent flyer miles—for her seat, and she is entitled to every millimeter of it!

THE FRIENDLY SKIES: Do your best to make sure that your movements don't disturb others. Avoid fidgeting, and be careful not to step on anyone's feet when getting in and out of your seat (by all means, politely ask your neighbor to stand so that you don't have to climb over him). Usually, there are not only people next to you, but in front and back of you as well. Refrain from kicking the seat in front of you, and be gentle when putting your seat back or folding up your tray.

KEEP IT TO YOURSELF: When using headphones (whether watching a movie or listening to music), keep the volume down so as not to bother those around you. Your neighbors should not be able to hear the sound coming from your listening device.

COOL YOUR JETS: At the end of a flight, passengers often begin gathering their belongings and jockeying for exit positions before the plane has come to a complete stop. Unless you are already late for a connection, wait your turn.

TRAINS *and* SUBWAYS

NO SNATCHING SEATS: While some passenger trains have assigned seating, most—especially commuter rails and subways—don't. Passengers who have been waiting the longest should board first, the exception being those who may need extra assistance.

GIVE IT UP: If an older or less able-bodied person needs a seat, you should always offer yours.

STAKING YOUR SPACE: Refrain from using an extra seat for your bags, feet, or wet umbrella. Not only does this prevent other passengers from sitting, but it leaves the seat wet and dirty.

CANCEL THAT CALL: Prolonged cell phone use in a situation where other individuals are trapped and forced to listen to you is not acceptable. If you must place a call with critical information—such as your arrival time—keep the conversation brief and your voice low. Ideally, you should not speak on your cell phone at all while on the train; text instead!

STINKY SITUATIONS: When trapped with other passengers in a small space, you should do all you can to avoid offending them. This includes bathing on a regular basis and using deodorant (which, of course, you should be doing anyway), keeping your shoes on, and not eating food with potent odors. If you do eat or drink on board, pick up after yourself.

AUTOMOBILES

DILIGENT DRIVER: As the driver, you must assume host duties in the car. This responsibility entails getting rid of any rubbish in advance, knowing how to get where you're going or being willing to ask for directions, and playing music that is acceptable to most of your passengers. Last but certainly not least, and this should go without saying, you must pay attention to the road and obey the laws for safe roadway travel.

THE PERFECT PASSENGER: As a passenger, you should avoid distracting the driver. And if you are a frequent passenger who isn't a member of the immediate family, you should offer money for gas or occasionally take the driver out to dinner.

OPENING DOORS: While on a business excursion, you should open the car door for any higher-ranking associate or any client. If you're on a date, opening the car door will score you some extra points in many cases. If your date is wearing an evening gown, help her into the car by extending your right hand so that she may steady herself. When she's exiting the vehicle, give her your right hand so that she may use it to help pull herself up.

ROAD RAGE: I would be remiss not to mention that road rage is rude. Honking excessively, making finger gestures, and shouting anything (including obscenities) at fellow drivers is not only unacceptable, but dangerous.

CHAPTER TEN

TIPS *on* TIPPING

TIPPING IS AN IMPORTANT PART OF OUR culture. The amount of a gratuity is based not only on the quality of service you receive, but also on your budget and the region in which you live. (If you're finding that your budget is really stretched when you hit the end-of-year tipping season, or you are always counting out change to cover the tip, you may be living a little beyond your means.) The following guidelines for gratuity amounts are general; consult local resources for numbers that are specifically appropriate for the area in which you live.

OUT *and* ABOUT

RESTAURANTS

MAÎTRE D': $10 to $50 for a special table, complicated reservation, or large party

COAT CHECK: $1 to $2 per item

WAITPERSON: 15 to 20 percent of the total bill (the busing staff receives a cut from this)

SOMMELIER: 8 to 15 percent of the wine bill

BARTENDER: $1 to $5 per drink when at the bar

RESTROOM ATTENDANT: $1—even if he doesn't hand you a towel (he's there to make sure that everything stays tidy)

BUFFET/COUNTER SERVICE: 10 percent of the bill

PERSONAL CARE

BARBER/HAIRSTYLIST: 15 to 20 percent of the cost for services

COLORIST: 15 to 20 percent of the cost for services

SHAMPOO PERSON: $1 to $10, depending on how much she's done (some give scalp massages and mini facials)

FACIALIST: 10 percent

MANICURIST: 10 to 15 percent

PEDICURIST: 15 to 20 percent

MASSEUSE: 10 percent

PHYSICAL THERAPIST: no tip, but do give an end-of-year gift

CHILD CARE

BABYSITTER: tip when children have been especially taxing or if you arrive home later than expected

DAY CARE: no tip, but give an end-of-year gift

MOVERS AND SHAKERS

MOVERS: $10 to $50 per mover, depending on the size of the move, the number of steps, and the number of heavy pieces

LAWN/SNOW CREW: no tip until the end of the year (see page 143)

CLEANING PERSON: if you've just had a big party or you've requested special services, $10 to $50 beyond what you agreed to pay

GROCERY BAGGER: $1 per bag if this person has brought the bags to your car (only done in certain locales)

LICENSED REPAIR PERSON: no tip

BUILDING SUPERINTENDENT: $3 to $20, depending on the issue and time of day

DELIVERY PEOPLE: $1 to $5 for flowers, balloons, pizza, and other food deliveries; employees of large shipping companies are not tipped

NEWSPAPER DELIVERY PERSON: 50¢ to $1 a week, or $20 to $50 at the end of the year (how good is his aim?)

DOG WALKER: $10 if he also takes in the mail or waters plants for a week, or whatever you deem appropriate if he intervenes in a pet emergency

TAXI DRIVER: 10 to 15 percent provided you weren't taken on an unrequested tour of the city

LIMOUSINE DRIVER: 15 to 20 percent unless the tip is already included (be sure to check)

TIPPING VIA TECHNOLOGY

Do be aware that computer coders are not always etiquette experts. In many venues, including restaurants and salons, as well as taxis, you will have the option of adding the tip to your credit card. Often the percentages are 15%, 20%, or 25% when the choice should be 10% or 20%. Do not feel bullied by the technology to give more than appropriate. Educate yourself to avoid overtipping.

TRAVEL TIPPING

BELLHOP: $1 to $2 per bag

MAID: $1 to $2 per person per night (left on a pillow on the bed, so that it's clear the money is for the maid)

ROOM DELIVERY: $1 to $2

ROOM SERVICE: 15 to 20 percent, unless already included (be sure to check)

DOORMAN: no tip to open the door or guide you to a taxi waiting at a stand; $1 to 10 to flag down a cab for you, depending on the weather

VALET: $2 to $5 when the car is dropped off and another $2 to $5 when the car is picked up

CONCIERGE: $5 to $10 for a special service such as acquiring tickets to a sold-out show, or obtaining last-minute dinner reservations for a local hot spot

TOUR GUIDE: $1 to $10 per person per day

END *of* THE YEAR

The end of the year is your chance to show your appreciation for those who make your life easier. How much to give is highly subjective. Amounts depend upon your relationship with the person, local norms, and your financial capacity. Bills should be new and crisp, and placed in an envelope with a card or a note of appreciation. When appropriate, a small gift may be given along with a monetary tip. Here are some general guidelines.

CHILD CARE

BABYSITTER: two nights' pay

NANNY: one week's salary for each year of service or, after the first year, 10 percent of yearly salary

AU PAIR: one week's salary for each year of service or, after the first year, 10 percent of yearly salary, and a small gift from the children

APARTMENT LIVING

CUSTODIAN: $20 to $100

DOORMAN: $25 to $200

HANDYMAN: $25 to $100

SUPERINTENDENT: $25 to $200

PARKING ATTENDANT: $20 to $100

HOME CARE

CLEANING PERSON: one week's salary

DOG WALKER: one week's pay

GARBAGE PERSON: $20 to $50

REGULAR DELIVERY PERSON (NEWSPAPER, DRY CLEANING, GROCERIES, ETC.): $5 to $50

LAWN/SNOW CREW: $10 per person, a bit more for the boss

PERSONAL CARE

The following are applicable if you're a regular customer.

BARBER/HAIRSTYLIST: cost of one session

COLORIST: cost of one session

SHAMPOO PERSON: $5 to $20

FACIALIST: cost of one session

MANICURIST/PEDICURIST: cost of one session

MASSEUSE: cost of one session

GIFTS INSTEAD OF GRATUITIES

The following individuals do not receive end-of-year tips; however, a small gift accompanied by a note of appreciation is appropriate.

MAIL CARRIERS

TEACHERS

LICENSED REPAIR PEOPLE SUCH AS PLUMBERS AND ELECTRICIANS

PHYSICAL THERAPISTS

DAY CARE PROVIDERS

///

CHAPTER ELEVEN

KEEP *in* TOUCH

\\\

WHEN WE THINK ABOUT INTERACTIONS, face-to-face encounters tend to come to mind. But in today's world, the vast majority of communication does not take place in person. Instead, we talk on the telephone, we text by mobile, we correspond via e-mail, we post on social media, and some of us even still enjoy the old-fashioned art of writing letters (and I think we all enjoy receiving those). As with any other type of interaction, these exchanges of thoughts, ideas, and information are likely to go more smoothly if you adhere to certain accepted guidelines.

INCOMING CALLS

THREE-RING CIRCUS: You should answer the phone when you hear the third ring. Any earlier, and you're likely to startle the person (and you risk creating the impression that you have nothing better to do than sit by the phone). Any later, and you're bound to have an impatient caller on your hands.

SCREEN AWAY: It is indeed acceptable to screen your calls. You have a life, after all, and the caller should not expect you to stop whatever you're doing to answer the phone. In fact, it may actually be more efficient to let the machine or voice mail pick up; for instance, if the caller has a specific question, you can be prepared with the answer when you return the call.

AGAIN WITH THE SMILE: Have you noticed a recurring theme here? When you answer the phone, you should smile so that you sound happy to speak to the caller. Even though the caller may not be able to see you, that smile will come through in your voice.

FULLY EQUIPPED: There should be something to write on and something to write with next to every telephone so that you can take notes and messages as necessary. You should not make the person on the other end of the line wait while you dig around for a writing implement or a piece of paper. And, of course, once you've taken a message, make sure that it is delivered to the appropriate person.

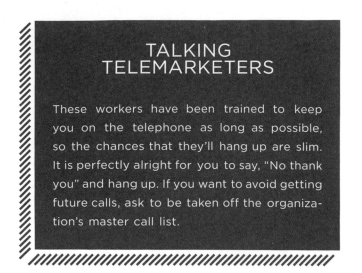

TALKING TELEMARKETERS

These workers have been trained to keep you on the telephone as long as possible, so the chances that they'll hang up are slim. It is perfectly alright for you to say, "No thank you" and hang up. If you want to avoid getting future calls, ask to be taken off the organization's master call list.

MESSAGES 101: If you pick up the phone and the person who the caller is trying to reach is not available, politely offer to take a message. Be sure to note the person's full name, her telephone number, and any brief message. Even if the caller doesn't wish to leave a message, you should let the intended recipient of the call know who phoned.

THE OUTGOING MESSAGE: The outgoing greeting on your answering machine or voice mail should help inform callers that they've reached the correct number and should last no longer than thirty seconds.

THE VOICE MAIL VOID: People who leave you a message should not feel like they're talking into a black hole. Check your voice mail or machine frequently, and return messages promptly. While you should return a call within twenty-four hours in the business world, there's a bit more leeway when it comes to your social life. If the message is important, call back as soon as possible, but if a friend is just phoning to shoot the breeze, you can wait a few days if you're busy.

CALL WAITING: Unless you're expecting an urgent call (in which case you should forewarn the person you're speaking to), you should not answer your call waiting; let it ring through to voice mail instead. If you don't have voice mail, get it or get rid of call waiting. In the interim, if you absolutely must pick up, make it snappy and tell the second caller you'll phone him back. Unless it's an emergency, you should not hang up on the first call in favor of the second; doing so would be extremely rude.

OUTGOING CALLS

PROPER I.D.: The person who initiates the call is required to identify himself first. (If you receive a call from someone who launches into the conversation without letting you know who's speaking, you should not hesitate to ask who it is.)

TAKE IT SLOW: When leaving a message, speak slowly and enunciate. Provide both your name and phone number twice, and give a brief account of your purpose for calling. You want to make it as easy as possible for your call to be returned.

BE COURTEOUS: Before picking up the telephone at midnight, think about who you are calling, both schedule and time zone. If she keeps a vampire's schedule, then go ahead. But if you know that she's an early riser, it is better to hold off until the next day. In instances when you aren't sure whether it's a safe time to call someone, wait until you're certain that it's alright and that you won't be disturbing anyone.

ALL CALLS

BACKGROUND NOISE: There are a lot of sounds that can be heard over the telephone—from typing to chewing to flushing. Avoid such activities while on the phone. It is impolite not to be giving your full attention to the person with whom you're speaking.

GRACEFUL GOOD-BYES: If the person you're talking to is a bit of a chatterbox and you need to get off the phone, saying something as simple as, "I am so glad we had the chance to speak today" or "I'd like to talk longer, but I've really got to run" can help bring the conversation to a smooth close without offending the other person.

CRADLE WITH CARE: When hanging up the phone, do so gently. Avoid slamming the receiver down, as the resulting sound will be extremely unpleasant to the person on the other end if he still has the phone by his ear.

For information specific to telephone etiquette in the business world, see page 169.

CELL PHONE CONDUCT

THE TWO V'S: When the sound of a ring might disturb others, either turn off your cell phone and let calls go directly to voice mail or set it on vibrate. If you switch your phone to vibrate, refrain from answering it when you're in any situation where speaking on the phone would disturb others. For instance, if you're at a restaurant, the movies, the theater, a wedding, or a funeral, you should not take a call.

PLAN B: If someone is really going to need to reach you and you don't have a vibrate setting on your phone, you should give the person an alternate way of contacting you. For instance, if you'll be at a restaurant, provide the main number and address of that establishment in case of emergency.

RUDE RESPONSES: If you are in the company of others—at a party or other gathering, on a date, or on an interview— your attention should be devoted to them. You should not answer your cell phone.

CONFIDENTIAL CONVERSATIONS: If you're speaking on your cell phone while out and about, your conversation can be overheard. If the topic of your discussion should not be made available for public consumption, postpone the call until you have privacy.

BANISHED FROM BELTS: Clipping your cell phone to your belt is a fashion faux pas. These communication devices should be kept out of sight in a pocket or briefcase.

from CLUELESS *to* CLASS ACT

MOBILE MESSAGING

QUICK 'N' EASY: Texting is a wonderful way to communicate when you have to send someone a message fast: an address for a meeting, that you will arrive in five, or the final color choice from a client. A prolonged conversation, upsetting news, or something subjective should be carefully considered before being sent via text.

EMOT-AWAY: When swapping texts with friends and family, emoticons are a great way to express your emotions. They are a wonderful way to add tone to your words. But just like salt in cooking, a little can go a long way. If you have more icons than text, it is time to rethink what you are trying to say. And only in the most extreme situations would you use emoticons in professional communiqués.

CLUMSY THUMBS: As with all messages, there is an ease in forwarding, which means we need to apply extra caution when sending something off to be sure what we are saying is appropriate *and* that it is being sent to the intended recipient.

NEVER HIDE: It is easy to hide behind our electronic devices. Be the bigger person: if there is a conversation that needs to be had, call or speak to the person face-to-face. Sending texts to avoid an interaction is simply poor form.

BE GONE: As with all tools, there are times when you should use them and times when they must be put away. Stop texting and turn off your mobile device when you should be interacting with others. Do not use your phone as an electronic security blanket to mask a lack of social skills.

E-MAIL ETIQUETTE

NO SHORTCUTS: Yes, e-mail is a fast and easy means of communication, but do not get lazy about it or regress to your old elementary school habits. Use capital letters at the beginning of your sentences and at the beginning of proper names (it is extremely disrespectful to start someone's name with a lowercase letter). Check your spelling, and since spellcheck does not catch every type of error, proofread before you hit send.

MASS MISSIVES: Occasionally, you will need to send out the same information to a number of individuals. Protect their privacy and contact information. When e-mailing more than three people who do not know one another, use the blind carbon copy (bcc) field for their addresses.

TONE-DEAF: Be careful of not only what you write, but the way you write it. Tone can be highly difficult to interpret in an e-mail, so try to be as clear as possible. Refrain from using all capital letters, as this is considered YELLING. If there's a word or phrase that you'd like to stress, place an asterisk on either side of it for *emphasis.*

BREAK DOWN THE BARRIERS: Because tone can easily be misinterpreted in an e-mail and issues are often complex, many problems are better resolved by talking face-to-face or on the phone. Do not hide behind your computer to avoid what might be a difficult interaction.

TRUE OR FALSE: Before forwarding an e-mail that promises free merchandise or warns against some horrible future occurrence, make sure that the content is accurate. There are countless false statements and offers circulating in cyberspace.

CONSIDER THE CONTENT: If you have e-mail at work, think twice about the information you are sending and your intended recipient. E-mail is considered the property of the employer and may be monitored. Some organizations specifically forbid the use of e-mail for personal matters. For this reason, you also shouldn't send e-mail of a personal nature to someone's workplace if that individual has not indicated that it is alright to do so.

TURNAROUND TIME: Unlike in the business world, where a one- or two-day turnaround is expected, you have up to a week to respond to e-mail sent by friends and family (unless they've specifically requested a more prompt reply, in which case you should try to accommodate).

HANDS OFF THE HANDHELD: You may think you are being sooo discreet typing away under the table, but you are only fooling yourself. Checking and sending e-mail with a handheld device while you're in the company of others should be undertaken with care and only when absolutely necessary (for instance, if you're under strict orders from your boss to do so). When you're with others, your focus should be on personal, not electronic, interactions.

For information specific to e-mail etiquette in the business world, see page 170.

SOCIAL MEDIA MANNERS

PERFECTLY PRIVATE: You may adjust all the settings you want, but there is nothing private once it has been posted. Status updates and pictures, once posted, can be copied and pasted or forwarded without your knowledge or permission.

CREATE BOUNDARIES: In the world of social media, there are many options. Ideally you will have one platform for your business contacts and connections, and a separate platform for friends and family.

PR AGENTS: In the world of social media, you are your own public relations agent. Take this role seriously and carefully consider what you post. Not everyone cares about the mundane details of your daily life, nor do they want to read a creative writing exercise about the highlife you are living. A bit of humor and a bit of humility can make your posts infinitely more readable.

POLITICAL POSTINGS: You certainly have every right to your opinion. Your friends and followers will afford your posting greater gravity when they are informed and respectful. Do not engage in a war of words . . . especially on someone else.

BE SENSITIVE: While not everyone can be included in every dinner, event, or gathering, you do want to take care that feelings are not hurt when others, who are reading your posts, are not included in the festivities.

LOG INTO LIFE: If perusing everyone's posts is making you long for a more exciting life, trust your gut. Log off the computer and get out there. Meet friends for dinner, catch up with college roommates, plan a party, or book a vacation.

LETTER WRITING

PAPER PRODUCTS: Ideally, letters should be written on stationery or note cards. There is something to be said for the more formal, luxurious feeling of high cotton-fiber content in watermarked paper. For informal correspondence, an amusing note card can lift the spirits.

PERSONALIZE IT: It is a good idea to acquire personalized stationery, which can bear your full name, your first name, or your monogram. The envelope may be left blank or bear your address on the back flap. Personalized paper can be ordered from most stationery stores, copy centers, or individual dealers. You should try to order note cards (folded or not) for brief pieces of correspondence and thank-you notes, as well as writing sheets for more formal correspondence. Keep in mind that the higher the percentage of cotton fiber, the nicer the paper. When it comes to printing techniques, engraved stationery is the most formal (and expensive), but thermography offers a similar look at a lower cost.

TYPING VS. WRITING: If you are composing a long letter, or you have horrid penmanship, typing may be the logical choice. However, short notes, thank-you notes, condolence notes, and love letters really should be handwritten. Handwriting is more personal. If you must print, choose a handwritten font and be sure to sign your missive.

PROPER PEN: Letters should be written with a pen, as pencil has a tendency to smudge and fade. The more formal the note, the darker the ink color. For those of you who have yet to try a fountain pen, there is something very sensual about using one on high-quality writing paper.

TAKE YOUR TIME: A well-written letter is never rushed. Think about where the recipient is, what she is doing, and what the two of you have in common. You may even wish to compose the letter on scrap paper first to avoid making mistakes on your good stationery. If you are a few lines into a long letter, or are proofreading a note, and spot a mistake, you may cross out the error and write your correction neatly above it or in the margin. While this would be unacceptable in business, there is a bit more flexibility in social correspondence.

SPELLING MADE SIMPLE: When writing a letter, all words must be spelled properly. The dictionary is your friend. Use it.

GRAMMAR: You should also take care to use proper grammar when writing a letter. If you have trouble in this area and are sending an important piece of correspondence, ask someone with a better feel for grammar to read a draft. Sometimes, just reading the letter out loud will help you to catch any mistakes.

SIGN-OFFS AND SIGNATURES: Like all good things, all good letters must come to an end. The way in which you bring your piece of correspondence to a close will depend upon the nature of the letter and your relationship with the recipient. Typical sign-offs include: "Sincerely," "Best regards," "Warm regards," "Yours truly," and "Love" (of these, "Sincerely" is the most formal). And, of course, don't forget to sign your name.

STAYING CONNECTED

It is interesting to note that people who are successful, both socially and professionally, devote a good deal of energy to keeping in touch. They do not call only when they want something. They call to catch up or share some information that they think the other person might find interesting or useful. They write birthday cards and thank-you notes. They send articles that made them think of the other person. They pass along names of people, books, and restaurants. They understand that building friendships, networks, and support structures takes time and effort. Keeping in touch and maintaining relationships is a lifelong success skill—and anyone can do it.

CONDOLENCE
NOTES

EVERY MOMENT COUNTS: You should write (not type) a condolence note as soon as you learn of a death. The longer you put it off, the harder it will become. If you end up putting it off for a bit, you should still send a note. It is important for the mourners to know that you care.

CONSIDERATE CONTENT: What exactly you write will vary depending on your relationship with the deceased as well as your relationship with the person to whom you are writing. Keep the focus of the note on the deceased and your thoughts of the living. If you knew the deceased, you might want to share one of your treasured memories of this person.

Dear Mrs. Matthews,

I was saddened to learn of your husband's passing. We frequently worked together on projects. His wry sense of humor enabled us to endure long, tedious meetings with difficult clients.

My deepest condolences,
Aaron Lesley

Dear Cousin Max,

As you know, I never met Andrea's mother, but from the stories you recounted, I could tell she was a remarkable woman. I was especially impressed with her ability to teach young children table manners through games and jokes. You and your family are in my thoughts and prayers.

Love,
Zach

WORDS TO AVOID: Everyone copes with loss in a different way. Telling a mourner how she should feel, how lucky she is, or that the death was "for the best" truly does not help her feel any better.

THANK-YOU NOTES

WHEN TO WRITE: If someone took the time to give you a gift, you should take the time to write that person a note expressing your gratitude (it's the least you can do, and it's not that difficult). You should also write a thank-you note when someone has made an extra effort on your behalf, such as referring a client to you, hosting a meal, or getting you an interview for a job. And whenever you have interview, you should send a thank-you note to the rviewer. All thank-you notes should be sent as soon ssible.

ND-SUSPENDERS THANKS: There are times uick e-mail thank-you is important to let the per- the gift arrived or that you appreciated the interview. Shortly thereafter the official handwritten thank-you note is sent to express your heartfelt gratitude for their thoughtfulness and time.

THE PERSONAL TOUCH: Thank-you notes should be handwritten—in ink of course. This has a warmer effect than typing.

BETTER LATE THAN NEVER

It is never too late to write a personal thank-you note. Yes, you should write the note as soon as possible—within a few days of a gift-giving holiday and within a week of a birthday party, for example. But even if you have gone beyond the proper time frame, you still need to send a note. You should apologize for your tardiness, but don't give excuses. The later the note is sent, the longer it will need to be (so do it when you're supposed to)!

WON'T A CALL DO? People often hope that merely saying thank you in person or over the phone absolves them of any obligation to write a thank-you note. Yes, there are occasions when a verbal thank-you is fine—when a friend gives you a magazine he's finished reading, when your mother mails you the tie you left during your visit home, or when a buddy remembers to e-mail you the phone number of the gym you wanted to join. But when you are given a gift, taken out for a nice meal, or given a professional reference, you must put pen to paper.

WHAT TO SAY: Sincerity is the most important aspect in writing a thank-you note. Mention the gift or action specifically, and let the recipient know why you appreciated it. Here are some examples to set you off on the right track.

Dear Marianne,

It was so nice of you to remember my birthday! Thank you so much for the daily planner. As you know, I have a difficult time staying organized. This gift will certainly be a big help.

Yours truly,
Nicolas

Dear Allen,

Lunch was fantastic! Thank you so much for treating me to a meal outside the office. The food was great, and I enjoyed catching up. I look forward to reciprocating in the near future.

Best regards,
Jeff

//

CHAPTER TWELVE

LIFE
at
WORK

\\\

NAVIGATING THE POLITICAL SCENE AT work is never easy. Because some rules and practices vary depending on the industry or individual company, you'll need to take your cues from those around you and modify your actions accordingly. However, there are some standards with regard to conduct that you should know and follow. The more professional and polished your behavior, the better off you'll be in your career.

CAPABLE CLOTHING

LOOK THE PART: People do make judgments about ability based on appearance. Make the best impression possible by looking polished and professional at all times, even if your office is business casual.

ALTERING FOR THE INTERVIEW: When applying for any job, you want to be your best self. But do not pretend to be someone you are not. If you hate suits, don't interview for a job where suits are daily attire. If you love your beard, find a company where facial hair is considered acceptable. DJing gigs will consider visible tattoos a plus whereas a bank might find tongue piercings off-putting. There are many corporate cultures out there; find the one to match your personality.

KNOW THE CODE: Before you start a new job, ask about the dress code. Your first clue should have been what the people who interviewed you were wearing at the time. Many companies have highly detailed, written dress codes and some even have "look books" with examples. Appropriate office attire varies based on the industry, the geographic region, the individual company, and even the different departments within a company. Typically, finance is a conservative field, whereas fashion and entertainment are more casual and trendy. Your ability to determine what is appropriate for your position will contribute to your success.

If you are planning to climb the corporate ladder, you should dress for the job you desire, not the job you have. You want people, especially management, to be able to envision you easily in the next role. Be careful, though, not to overdo it. One notch above your peers is usually sufficient.

ALWAYS OVER: Whether you're heading to a workplace for your first day on the job or going to a meeting with a new client, when in doubt, it is always better to be overdressed than underdressed. Men have a distinct advantage over women, since they can always remove their tie, unbutton their top button, or take off their suit coat for a more casual look if, in the end, the situation calls for it.

The DAILY GRIND

WEAR A WATCH: Keeping your eye on the time is important. You should arrive for meetings, and work in general, a few minutes before you are due.

LATE ARRIVAL: If you are running late for an appointment, call ahead to let the other party know that you're on your way. When you arrive, make your entrance as unobtrusive as possible. When appropriate, apologize, but do not rationalize or offer excuses. Allow the discussion to stay focused on business—you don't want to waste any more of the other party's time.

BE EQUIPPED: When heading to a meeting, be sure to bring any necessary background paperwork, paper and writing implements for taking notes, and business cards (you don't need the latter if the only people at the meeting are your coworkers). You want to inspire confidence in those around you—not appear to be ill-prepared or disorganized.

COMPUTER KEYS: As tempting as it may be to bring your laptop to every meeting, take care that it is relevant to the meeting at hand. Others will quickly know if you are working on something else, or worse, surfing the Web.

KEEP YOUR COOL: While a colleague might make you want to scream, don't. Take some time to cool off, gather your composure, and reassess the situation. Organizations have long memories for bad behavior and outbursts.

BE DIPLOMATIC: Undoubtedly, you and your colleagues will have differences of opinion regarding how a certain matter should be handled. Assuming you are in a position to speak up, you need to convey your point diplomatically. In other words, you need to disagree without being disagreeable. The way in which you express your disagreement will have a powerful effect on how your point of view is received.

BE DISCREET: While your frustration at work might make you want to vent, find the appropriate avenue. A close confidant with a sympathetic ear is a significantly better option than posting anything online as the latter can be grounds for dismissal.

COURTESY TO ALL: Treat all fellow employees with respect, regardless of where they stand in the company hierarchy. Present a professional face to everyone.

THE ROAD TO SUCCESS

I cannot count how many times I have interacted with potential clients before actually meeting them. I have opened doors for them, smiled at them in hallways, and exchanged pleasantries in elevators, only to find out later that these were the very people I was in the building to meet. Extending such simple courtesies can help start a relationship on the right foot. Being impolite, on the other hand, can cause doors to slam in your face. In one instance, a management recruit was so rude to a relocation assistant that his lucrative job offer was rescinded. The employer wanted an executive who was kind to everyone—not just those at the top.

from CLUELESS *to* CLASS ACT

OFFICE BUDDIES: While you should take care to be friendly with everyone at work, you should also take care to build true friendships slowly. You will be spending much of your waking hours with your colleagues, but remember to have some boundaries between your personal and your professional lives. Not everyone who is friendly to you at work is actually your friend.

BE YOUR BOSS'S PR PERSON: Regardless of your feelings toward your boss, it is important to make him look good to other members of the team and to clients. Part of your job is to make sure that your boss is informed of important matters and is never caught by surprise.

SET EXPECTATIONS: Whether working with fellow employees or clients, it is important to realistically estimate the scope and time frame for your portion of any project. You should give yourself extra time for delays and emergencies that may arise. Whenever possible, complete your portion ahead of schedule so that others know they can rely on you.

NETWORKING VS. IDLE CHATTER: While being known as the office gossip is not good for your career, hiding in your office is also a mistake. It is important for you to be aware of what is happening in your workplace. You should know who the important players are and make sure they know you. Get up from your desk and make plans with colleagues for lunch. You might even join a company sports team or help with a company-sponsored charity event to meet and get better acquainted with others in the organization.

SELECTIVE LISTENING: For those who work in an open office environment, selective listening is a must. As tempting as it may be to eavesdrop on your coworkers, you need to be able to tune out other people so that you can get your own job done. If you absolutely can't help but overhear, under no circumstances should you interject yourself into the conversation or give advice on the matter later.

KEEP IT DOWN: When on the phone or having a discussion with others—whether personal or private—don't be excessively loud; undoubtedly there are others around you who need to be able to concentrate on what they're doing. If listening to the radio is permitted in your workplace, keep the volume low, or better yet, opt for an earbud.

WERE YOU RAISED IN A BARN? At the office, it is necessary to pick up after yourself. From throwing away the bag that your lunch came in to picking up your coffee cup when you leave a meeting, you need to be tidy. If there's an office kitchen, don't leave your dirty dishes lying around on the counter or in the sink. And if you spill something, wipe it up!

REFRIGERATOR RIGHTS: It should go without saying, but don't help yourself to food that doesn't belong to you in a common fridge. You also shouldn't leave your own food in the fridge for too long—others should not be subjected to the stench of your spoiled leftovers.

YOU ARE THE COMPANY: Anytime you make contact with someone outside the office, you represent the company for which you work. Whether you are communicating in person, over the phone, or through written correspondence, you should be as polished as possible. Avoid slang, misspellings, and any remarks that may be a bit too casual for a business interaction.

HOLIDAY GIFT GIVING: Many companies have specific guidelines regarding gift giving. Check the employee handbook. If you can't find your answer there, ask a fellow employee.

PROFESSIONALISM *and the* PHONE

TEST DRIVE: After you've recorded your outgoing message on your voice mail or answering machine, listen to it to make sure it sounds professional.

KEEP IT CURRENT: If you leave a dated or special outgoing greeting, update it as needed. If you will be away or unable to check your voice mail for more than seventy-two hours, you should mention that on your outgoing message. When possible, you should also provide an alternate contact.

FOREWARN BEFORE FORWARDING: When passing a call on to another person, be sure to tell the caller the name and number of the person to whom you're transferring her (the latter piece of information is a precaution in case the line gets disconnected). Before you put the call through to the next person, let that individual know who the caller is and the reason for the call.

EXIT STAGE RIGHT: There tends to be an inverse relationship between the chattiness of one party and the workload of the other. Here are a few lines to help politely bring a phone conversation to a close: "Thank you for your time—I will look into this now"; "I will follow up with you on this matter by the end of next week, thank you so much for calling"; "This input is very valuable to us and we truly appreciate your bringing it to our attention."

For more information on phone etiquette, see pages 146–150.

BUSINESS E-MAIL

BE SPECIFIC: The subject line is your friend. Write brief, descriptive titles. This will not only alert the recipient to the matter at hand before opening, but also enable him to find the message easily if there is a need to refer back to it.

CC CONSERVATIVELY: Think carefully about who needs to see the information in any specific e-mail. You don't want to waste people's valuable time if the message isn't really pertinent to them.

DON'T CRY WOLF: Prioritize your e-mail appropriately. If you send everything high-priority, the little red exclamation point will begin to lose its meaning.

BE YOURSELF: Don't assume that the recipient will know who you are or be familiar with your organization. You may need to identify your title and company.

OBEY THE RULES: In the office, e-mail is a professional tool. The messages in your mailbox should be work related. Many companies reserve the right to monitor your workplace e-mail, with or without your knowledge

BE POLITE: As more and more of our daily work occurs over the Internet, an increasing number of our professional relationships will exist only over the Web. Strive to make every interaction a pleasant one.

For additional information regarding e-mail etiquette, see pages 152–154.

GRACIOUS GOOD-BYES

I QUIT! While it is tempting to include a manifesto of the company's ills in your resignation letter, you are better served by keeping such thoughts to yourself and making the content as simple as possible. A resignation letter needs only three elements: the date of your last day working for the company, your contact information (address, e-mail, and phone number), and your signature.

STRATEGIC TIMING: Once you have decided that you are going to leave a company, you often become a lame duck. Plan the times of your announcement and final departure carefully. Be sure to factor in time for a replacement to be found and some training to take place, but do not linger. Most companies have a standard resignation time frame.

Read your company manual carefully before submitting your resignation. Also, take into consideration the company culture. Some organizations have a stated two-week notice for resignations but will escort you to the door the day you submit your letter.

FAREWELL FESTIVITIES: In some instances, your employer or boss might throw you a going-away party. However, you are not allowed to plan your own. Your exit could be more political than you think, and your former coworkers will need to ally themselves with the organization. If you have a few close friends from work, you might arrange to meet them for dinner outside the office, but don't announce your plans to the entire group.

EXIT INTERVIEWS: Many companies interview outgoing employees to gather information. Answer all questions judiciously. Some exit interviews are confidential, while others are not. In addition, you don't want to burn any bridges. Boomerang employees (ones who leave a company only to be hired back a few years later) are becoming more and more common.

IT'S A SMALL WORLD: If you specialize in a certain field, it is highly probable that you and the people you are leaving behind will cross paths in the future. Keep relationships positive and communication open. You never know when you might see (or need) your former superior or coworkers.

TAKE THE HIGH ROAD: Not only is it less crowded, but you're less likely to regret something that you said or did. Leaving a company can be stressful and unnerving, but you need to keep your wits about you. Don't yell at anyone, don't destroy company property, don't take office supplies, and don't disparage the organization to clients, the media, or others in the field. Doing so will only reflect negatively on you.

---

* Throughout this book I have referred to dating situations in terms of the traditional male and female dynamic. Nowadays we live in a world where there are a range of gender identifications as well as romantic relationships. The text in the initial revision with gender inclusiveness quickly became quite convoluted, cumbersome, and difficult to comprehend. For clarity and for brevity an editorial decision was made to use either "he" or "she" for a particular example.

CONCLUSION

Clients often cringe when I tell them I love to read antique etiquette books for fun. But these instructional guides—which offer snapshots of the time in which they were written—have the power to transport me to a different era. Discussing such matters as how to send a well-written mailgram and how a gentleman should tip his hat when meeting a lady on the street, these books from yesteryear open a window to another world. Yet as I travel back in time via the yellowing pages of these tomes, I realize that the more things change, the more they stay the same. While we no longer leave calling cards at people's homes or send letters of introduction with friends moving to new cities, the underlying principles remain constant. Etiquette is about respecting yourself and showing respect toward others. It is about having confidence in yourself and making those around you feel comfortable. No matter what the era, if you know what behaviors are appropriate in any given situation, you are able to relax and enjoy yourself. When you relax, you put others at ease. And, when you put others at ease, they enjoy being with you.

Etiquette is fascinating because it involves so many different areas: history, sociology, psychology, gender issues, race relations, and technology. It is my hope that this book has not only helped you to conduct yourself in a more polished way, but also sparked some curiosity and interest in you regarding human behavior.

INDEX

Airplanes, manners on, 135–136
Alcohol, drinking, 81–83
Attire. *See also* Shoes
    appropriate, 103–104
    fine arts performance, 15
    formal, 105–110
    funeral, 23
    helping with her coat, 9, 14
    party, 29
    religious service, 19–20
    rock concert, 17–18
    wedding, 35–36
    work, 163–164
Automobile, courtesy in, 137–138

Babies
    arrival of/visiting, 126
    expectant couples and, 124–126
    gifts and showers, 125, 127
    new-parent manners and, 127
Bar basics, 9, 42–46
Bathroom use, 29, 32, 33, 47, 57
Book overview, 6
Breath, freshness of, 100–101

Cars, courtesy in, 137–138
Challenges, assisting people with, 128
Child care, tipping for, 140, 143
Church, attending, 19–21
Class act, becoming, 5–6
Clothing. See Attire
Cologne and fragrances, 102
Communication, 145–161
    cell phone etiquette, 17, 19, 67, 78, 134,
        137, 150
    condolence notes, 158–159
    conversation guidelines, 11–12, 48–49,
        112–117, 119
    e-mail, 152–153, 170–171
    letter writing, 155–157
    mobile messaging, 134, 151–153
    phone calls, 146–150, 169–170
    social media manners, 154–155
    taboo topics, 119
    thank-you notes, 33, 38, 156, 157, 159–161
    Condolences and funerals, 21–24, 156,
        158–159

Dating, 88–97
    asking someone out, 94–96
    ending relationship, 96–97
    finding right partner, 89–90
    first date, 91–93
    general guidelines, 93–94
    this book, genders and, 173n

Dietary restrictions, 26
Dining, 61–87. *See also* Restaurants
    alcohol intake and, 81–83
    beginning meal, 66–69
    bread and butter, 69–70
    cooling, cutting, and mixing, 72
    dating and, 93–94, 96
    eating and chewing, 70
    finishing/clean plates/clearing, 73–74
    flying/falling things, 72–73
    following the leader, 66
    helping women/VIPS with chair, 80–81
    napkin use, 67
    passing things around, 71
    posture, elbows and, 67
    seating arrangements and, 52, 53
    setting table for, 54–56
    sharing servings, 72
    spilling things, 73, 74–75
    table manners, 78–81
    tasting, seasoning, and condiments, 70–71
    teeth trouble (food in teeth), 79–80
    toasts, 77
    tricky foods and, 83–87
    unwanted food, bones, bugs, and trash,
        75–77
    utensil placement, use, and silent signals,
        54–56, 62–66, 68
Dinner parties, 51–53. *See also* Dining
Doors, courtesy at/with, 130–131

Elevator/escalator etiquette, 132–133
E-mail etiquette, 152–153, 170–171
Etiquette, importance of, 174
Expectant couples, etiquette of, 124–126
Eyeglasses, 78, 104

Fine arts performances, 15–17
Formal attire, 105–110
Funerals and condolences, 21–24

Gifts
    for babies, 125, 126, 127
    of condolence, 22–23
    end-of-year tips and, 143–144
    for hosts, 27–28, 31
    thank-you notes for, 156, 159–161
    wedding, 34–35, 38
    workplace and, 169
Glasses, barware, 43–46
Grooming, 100–102
Guests, guidelines for, 25–38.
    See also Parties, attending
    general guidelines, 26–29
    giving gifts, 27–28, 31

staying over, 31–33
thanking host, 33
weddings, 34–38

Hair and grooming, 100–102
Handicaps, assisting people with, 128
Handshakes, 115, 117–118
Hosting, guidelines for, 39–60
    bar basics, 42–46
    conversation guidelines, 48–49, 112–117
    dinner parties, 51–53
    ending gathering, 49
    final preparations, 47–48
    greeting guests, 47
    inviting guests, 46, 49–50
    overnight guests, 57–59
    participation and activities, 47–49
    pet protocol, 59–60
    planning (who, what, how much), 40–47
    unexpected guests, 42

Illness, etiquette of, 121–124
Invitations
    asking someone out, 94–96
    bringing others, 26–27
    overnight guests, 57
    party/gathering, 40, 46, 49–50
    pet protocol, 59–60
    reciprocating, 39
    RSVPs, 26, 29
    wedding, 34, 35–36

Meeting and greeting, 111–119
    conversation guidelines, 112–117
    handshakes, 115, 117–118
    shyness and, 117
    taboo topics, 119
Messaging. See Communication
Mosque, attending, 19–21

Nails and grooming, 100–102
Notes, writing. See Communication

Opera, other fine arts performances, 15–17
Overnight stays, as guest, 31–33
Overnight stays, as host, 57–59

Parties, attending
    arriving, 29–30
    attire, 29
    conversation guidelines, 112–117
    gifts for hosts, 27–28
    guidelines, 26–31
    leaving, 30–31
    mingling and conversing, 30
Parties, hosting. See Hosting, guidelines for
Personal appearance, 98–110. See also Attire
    grooming, 100–102
    improving image, 99–100
Personal care, tipping for, 140, 144

Pets, 27, 59–60
Phones. See Communication
Photographs, 36–37, 91
Pregnancy. See Babies
Public places and events, 7–24. See also
    Restaurants
    fine arts performances, 15–17
    funerals, 21–24
    religious services, 19–21
    rock concerts, 17–18
    seating courtesies, 15–17, 18
    sporting events, 18–19

Religious services, 19–21
Restaurants, 8–14
    children and, 12
    doggie bags, 14
    food and drink, 9, 10–11
    helping with her coat, 9, 14
    paying and tipping, 13–14, 140
    reservations, 8
    respecting others, 11
    seating courtesies, 9–10
    waitstaff interaction, 12–13
Revolving doors, 131
RSVPs, 26, 29

Services, tipping for, 139–144
Shoes, 103, 104, 110, 137
Sidewalk, navigating, 134
Social media manners, 154–155
Subways and trains, 136–137
Synagogue, attending, 19–21

Table manners, 78–81
Table, setting, 54–56
Temple, attending, 19–21
Thank-you notes, 33, 38, 156, 157, 159–161
Tipping tips, 139–144
Toasts, 77
Trains and subways, 136–137
Transiting, manners and, 129–138
    airplanes, 135–136
    automobiles, 137–138
    doors (traditional and revolving), 130–131
    elevators/escalators, 132–133
    sidewalks and pedestrians, 134
    tipping and, 142–143
    trains and subways, 136–137
Tuxes/formal attire, 105–110

Weddings, 34–38
Work, life at, 162–175
    daily grind, 164–169
    dressing for, 163–164
    e-mail guidelines, 170–171
    leaving job, 171–173
    phone professionalism, 169–170
Worshipping, 19–21
Writing. See Communication